Few people speak with more eloquence and insight on the subject of euthanasia than Joni Eareckson Tada. *When Is It Right to Die?* offers a balanced and informed perspective.
    Elizabeth Dole

Why do those deemed unworthy by an increasingly self-centered culture possess a supposed "right to die," but other "unworthies," such as the unborn, are not endowed with the right to life? Joni Tada has not only thought through these things, she has lived through them and hers is a welcome and needed voice to the church and to the world.
    Cal Thomas, Syndicated Columnist

The book that Joni has just written, *When Is It Right to Die?*, is an urgently needed book for this moment of history. We commend it without reservation.
    Bill Bright

Understandably, Joni has suffered through tough times when she would have preferred to die. That makes her book compelling and persuasive. It should be read today—before "illness strikes and rational thinking goes out the window."
    Robert P. Dugan, Jr., Director
    National Association of Evangelicals

When Joni Eareckson, woman of God, advocate for the disabled, and chairbound quadriplegic discusses life's goodness, the time and way to die, and the black hole of euthanasia, her words carry weight.
    James Packer, Professor of Theology, Regent College

Arguments for "right to die" legislation seem chillingly reasonable. Joni counters the arguments to short-cut suffering with both careful thought and also a life of meaning and community woven from her personal experience with disability and despair. *When Is It Right to Die?* offers hope with integrity.
    Stephen A. Hayner, President
    InterVarsity Christian Fellowship

Joni Eareckson Tada has some genuine concerns about physician-assisted suicide. In this thought-provoking book, she provides her own considerations against euthanasia—openly and from the heart.
    Sandra Swift Parrino, Chairperson
    National Council on Disability

Joni's biblically radiant comments offer a welcome respite for today's bewildered society. *When Is It Right to Die?* grapples helpfully with the ethics, motivation, and process of constructive decision making.

Dr. Carl F. H. Henry
Evangelical Theologian and Author

With the "right to die" questions on so very many hearts and minds in these days, Joni addresses these moral and theological questions with great understanding, grace, and empathy. Both those who suffer—and those who minister to the suffering—will benefit greatly from this outstanding, timely book.

Ted W. Engstrom, President Emeritus
World Vision

I am moved by Joni's plea for wisdom. Truly humane law must be rooted in the deepest wisdom we can gain about the highest meaning of human life.

James W. Skillen, Executive Director
The Center of Public Justice

The "Right to Die" issues are not academic issues for Joni—she grapples with them daily and ministers to countless others who struggle continuously with life-and-death choices. Surely no one else could have made such a helpful or important contribution to the "Right to Die" discussion.

John MacArthur, Pastor

To share with God, even in our limited ways, is for each of us a "foreword" to the larger book of life. Joni shows us that death is not a "final exit," that it is not for us to end one phase of life, but to hold it in relation to God's larger purpose.

Myron S. Augsburger, President
Christian College Coalition

She directs us to know God in ways that few do and helps us to see that it is possible to know real life no matter what our circumstances. An important, rich, timely book from the heart of one who has met God.

Dr. Larry Crabb, Psychologist and Author

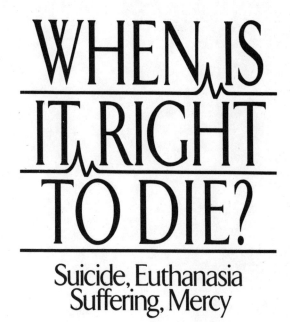

WHEN IS IT RIGHT TO DIE?

Suicide, Euthanasia Suffering, Mercy

Foreword by C. Everett Koop

WHEN IS IT RIGHT TO DIE?

Suicide, Euthanasia
Suffering, Mercy

JONI
EARECKSON TADA

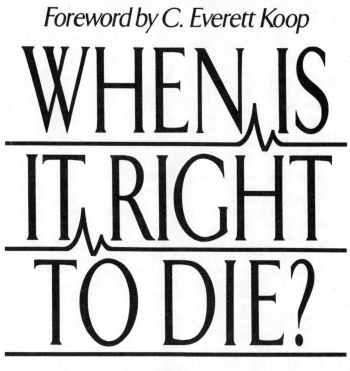

ZondervanPublishingHouse
Grand Rapids, Michigan

HarperSanFrancisco
San Francisco, California

Divisions of HarperCollinsPublishers

WHEN IS IT RIGHT TO DIE?
Copyright © 1992 by Joni Eareckson Tada
All rights reserved

Requests for information should be addressed to:
Zondervan Publishing House
Grand Rapids, Michigan 49530

Library of Congress Cataloging-in-Publication Data

Tada, Joni Eareckson.
    When is it right to die? : suicide, euthanasia, suffering, mercy /
Joni Eareckson Tada.
      p. cm.
    ISBN 0-310-58570-8 (acid-free paper)
    1. Suicide—Social aspects—United States. 2. Suicide—Religious
aspects—Christianity. 3. Euthanasia—Social aspects—United
States. 4. Euthanasia—Religious aspects—Christianity. 5. Right
to die—United States. 6. Handicapped—United States—Attitudes.
I. Title.
HV6548.U5T33   1992
362.2'8'0973—dc20   92–60215
                                                    CIP

Edited by John D. Sloan
Cover designed by Terry Dugan Design

Printed in the United States of America

92 93 94 95 96 / DH / 11 5 4 3 2

This edition is printed on acid-free paper and meets the American
National Standards Institute Z39.48 standard.

Vicky Olivas

John McAlexander

Debbie Stone

*Three people who have helped me
find life worth living.*

Contents

Foreword

Joni Eareckson Tada has written a timely, fresh discussion that speaks with a balanced voice to the question: When is it right to die? Not only does she address an issue being forced upon us as individuals, but one that has been suggested for a societal decision.

Joni speaks with a voice of one who has been there, who *is* there. She has known the uncertainty, the fear, the overwhelming truth, the despair, and the unendingness of a permanent disability. She has considered the options, discusses them openly from the heart, and shares with us her considered judgment. Those of us who are not in Joni's wheelchair may never be able to see the issues through Joni's eyes, but after reading this book we will see them more clearly than ever before.

Joni provides strong Christian, biblical arguments regarding euthanasia. But if you are not inclined to those authorities, remember that even though our society worships at the altar of high technology and seeks control of nature, the conquest of death will always elude us. Nevertheless, control over death is ever tempting.

Let those who seek death with dignity beware, lest they lose life with dignity in the process.

C. Everett Koop, M.D.
Surgeon General USPHS (1981–89)

Special Thanks

On this page you're invited to join in on an awards banquet where you can have a seat at the head table and listen to the accolades. If you're interested, stay and watch the plaques of recognition handed out. Sit awhile and listen to the speeches. These people whom I'm about to recognize are pretty special.

Francie Lorey and Judith Butler. These two deserve highest awards. They served as my hands in research and writing. They gave of their time, including Saturdays, and love to see this book completed.

Dr. John M. Frame. Only after I read his book *Medical Ethics: Principles, Persons, and Problems* was I convinced I could tackle the issue.

Dr. Nigel M. de S. Cameron of Trinity Evangelical Divinity School. His instruction and guidance in ethics guaranteed that this book would reflect sound judgment and solid morals.

David Neff, Managing Editor of *Christianity Today*. Whenever I wandered off the beaten path theologically or ethically, David was there to steer me back on course.

Dr. C. Everett Koop. Salt to our culture. Light to our nation. A prophet to the medical society, the legal establishment, the religious community, and to disabled persons and their families.

Steve Estes and Steve Jensen. Bless you for your help with research and editing. You both know how I feel.

John Sloan, my editor, and Scott Bolinder, my publisher. Thank you, and the rest of my friends at Zondervan, for giving focus, direction, and every resource needed to get the job done. Bless you for believing I had something to say. And yes, it's nice to be back with family again.

Michael and Georgie Lynch, along with the entire *JAF* staff. You helped keep things around the office going forward, even when my door was closed and the "Do Not Disturb" sign was hung out. Abundant thanks to the Monday lunch group for their constant encouragements.

My deepest appreciation goes to the people whose testimonies make up the backbone of this book. Their spirit has challenged me to face the moral judgments I must make with courage and conviction.

And the best for last, my husband Ken.

PART ONE

A Time to Live?

Let's Begin Here

I've never been one for dissertations.

Philosophy 101 at the University of Maryland? I barely squeezed by. Sitting under the austere gaze of a professor as he read his treatise in standard lecture-hall monotone? Forget it. My mind was already down at the college cafeteria checking out the menu. Oratory was for others, especially if it was dispensed in the language of computers, manuals, or big, heavy textbooks.

"Don't give me the *War and Peace* version. Just answer my questions." And as far as the following semester of philosophy was concerned, seriously now, did anybody really care that "I think, therefore I am"? A value system? Come on, wasn't right and wrong as easy to discern as black and white, night and day? Whether moralistic codes were situational or rigorously rigid was of little use to me. Just state the plain facts: Was it immoral? Illegal? Unethical? Just tell me.

Too often I refused to take the time or mental energy to hear and consider those answers. So what happened? I walked away thinking no meaningful answer existed.

It's far too easy to take a casual approach to looking for tough answers to even tougher questions. We go about our business and skirt along the edge of an emotional, ethical issue only to catch an occasional idea or two. Or perhaps it's not a lazy mental attitude at all. Maybe we're fearful of tough questions. Or we may be more frightened of the answers.

Somewhere along the line, however, our thinking shifts.

A debilitating accident has us grabbing the clergy by the collar to get them to testify to the rhyme or reason. A medical report has us up into the wee hours pouring over medical dictionaries to find the prognosis for osteogenesis imperfecta. An IRS audit has us studying tax forms, tax laws, and logging fifteen telephone calls into H&R Block to balance the figures. A teenage daughter gulps a bottle of pills and we stand shocked and slump-shouldered, wondering what to do. Suddenly the ethical issue we once skirted has pulled us in, and we simply cannot be satisfied until we find answers.

That is what happened to me.

A diving accident as a teenager left me totally, permanently paralyzed and in deadly despair . . . a cancerous tumor ate at my five-year-old niece's brain until she withered and wasted away . . . old age and a series of strokes gripped my ninety-year-old father in a web of tubes and machines.

Somewhere between those family tragedies, my thinking shifted and I was forced to face an issue I had too long ignored. Ethics was no longer confined to the classroom. Standards of moral judgment now had flesh and blood, life-and-death reality. Why not cut short the suffering, or have someone do it for you if the pain and agony of your disability is too great to bear? Why not leapfrog the dying process and mercifully end the life of a tortured little girl? Why not compassionately remove the plugs and let an old gentleman die? I had to find answers. That is, if there *were* answers.

It involved more than just my family's living nightmares. Twenty-five years in a wheelchair introduced me to the world of advocacy, and with it, thousands of disabled people who were either sinking into or surfacing out of suicidal despair. Decades of visiting hospitals and rehab centers introduced me to the business executive with Lou Gehrig's disease whose body was shrinking and shriveling, the young athlete paralyzed from a spinal cord injury and living in a nursing home, the Vietnam veteran coping with a strange new mental illness, and the teenager with cerebral palsy sitting on the sidelines, watching her classmates date and drive cars. Each of these, and thousands more, were periodically tempted to detour the extreme suffering or mental anguish by resorting to pills or a razor. And each one asked the same question: Why not end it all?

During my years as a national disability advocate,

I quickly saw how politicized these questions were becoming. I served on the National Council on Disability under President Reagan and then President Bush. I sat in the marbled chambers of government. I have listened to the "Why not end it all?" question batted back and forth like a tennis ball between politicians and legislators, doctors and handicap associations. I followed court rulings as the gavel was banged by the bedsides of comatose people. I kept an eye on the headlines every time aid-in-dying initiatives cropped up on state ballots.

Behind every newspaper story, every initiative on the ballot, every booklet printed by either a right-to-die or right-to-life group, was a family. A family like mine. A disabled person like me. A person, a family for whom my heart bled.

My heart went out to these people because I had been there. I had lived their story, as a severely depressed disabled person, as a family member, as a national advocate, and as a political activist. Their hurts were mine. Their pain I had felt in my own chest. Like them I had searched my own soul, wrestling with the toughest of ethical questions.

Questions that did, indeed, have answers. Although my depression seemed as paralyzing as my spinal cord injury, I had found an answer that made life worth living. Our family also found an answer for my suffering, cancer-ridden niece. And perhaps, most poignantly, there was even a touching answer for my dying father.

I became convinced that the same principles that

guided me and my family through the nightmarish maze of depression, suicide, and death could help others. What we had learned as a family could benefit other hurting families.

And that's the reason for the book you hold in your hands. Perhaps you are the quadriplegic in a wheelchair or the young mother of a little girl dying of a degenerative nerve disease. You may be sitting at the bedside of an elderly parent who is sinking deeper and deeper into dementia. Or maybe, just maybe, your life does not even touch the world of the terminally ill or dying or disabled. You are just plain tired of living for whatever painful reason. Your problems have piled on so high they only wear you down. Pain has become numbing. Your thinking has become clouded. You are tired, so very tired. Quiet desperation has settled in and you couldn't care less if there are answers. You only want the hurt to stop.

There is hope. An answer that you can live with is within reach. Now I don't want to come across as one of Job's comforters, dispensing pat answers that don't fit another person's problems. And don't worry; what you hold in your hands is not a college treatise.

This book is not about systems of ethics, but about people like you and me and the moral judgments we must make.

1

Painful Words

For years it's been music to my ears. "Joni, you don't look paralyzed at all. Why, you look like you could jump out of that wheelchair, pick up a tennis racquet, and stop 'em cold at the net."

Sounds nice. But sooner or later the inevitable was bound to happen. After twenty-five years of living in a wheelchair, my paralyzed body is beginning to break down. I shouldn't complain. I haven't suffered through the usual lung and kidney infections that accompany quadriplegia. I've enjoyed miraculously good health for years.

All that changed in 1991. For me it was a year of blood pressure problems, drastic weight loss, infections and worst of all, pressure sores on my sides and back. For three long weeks during that summer, two stubborn pressure sores forced me to bed. It wasn't easy lying flat and faceup. And who could guess how long it would take to close those oozing wounds? My last stint in bed with sores lasted two months!

In bed, nothing really changed but the days and, occasionally, the sheets. Thankfully I was able to keep my mind active writing an article or two and a few letters. My husband Ken hung a bird feeder outside our bedroom window, thinking the sparrows and occasional nasty blue jays would brighten my spirits. A squirrel he named Mr. McFizz came by daily for peanuts Ken tossed under the feeder. The birds and the business of writing the articles kept my mind active.

I tried to keep my heart active, too. Friends came by. I listened to cassette tapes. I watched a little television. All this kept depression at bay. Well, almost.

Because at times it was oh, so hard.

Like the day I began to feel claustrophobic, so hedged in. Being paralyzed, I couldn't stretch or toss and turn. It's not like I could hop out of bed for a few minutes, visit the refridge, stop by the bathroom and run a brush through my hair, then climb back under the sheets with a good book. Gravity was my enemy in bed. The only movement I could manage was to turn my head on the pillow. And after several weeks of lying stiff and still, I felt at that point I couldn't take any more. I had gone through enough.

Now I've survived years of physical setbacks and my faith has gotten me long past the bitter denial-bargaining-depression stage. But that didn't keep my mind from playing weird games. *I am tired, just plain worn out from living life with hands that don't work and feet that don't walk. I'm not pitying poor me, I'm just weary and ready to let go.*

I fought back tears and tried to focus on the sparrows fluttering around the feeder. *Maybe they'll cheer me up.* But not so. In fact, for a brief moment, I almost felt envious. *You birds have so much freedom, you can do as you please. No claustrophobic cages. No problems.*

I spent the rest of the afternoon staring at the ceiling, closed off from the chatter of the birds, and listening instead to the drip-drip of the urine that flowed from my tubing into the bedside bucket. My thoughts floated back to the early days of my paralysis in 1967, when I was hospitalized and in bed not just for three weeks but an entire year. Then my thin, gaunt frame was covered with pressure sores, and even though I was being force-fed, I could not gain weight. That meant even more sores. Thinking back, it amazed me that I endured an entire year of lying flat and faceup.

During those days, my depression wasn't mild or fleeting. I was gripped with the dull, lonely ache of despair. My personal holocaust was described in the book *Joni*:

> Here I was, trapped in this canvas cocoon. I couldn't move anything except my head. Physically, I was little more than a corpse. I had no hope of ever walking again. I could never lead a normal life and marry Dick. *In fact, he might even be walking out of my life forever*, I concluded. I had absolutely no idea of how I could find purpose or meaning in just existing day after day—waking, eating, watching TV, sleeping.

Why on earth should a person be forced to live out such a dreary existence? How I prayed for some accident or miracle to kill me. The mental and spiritual anguish was as unbearable as the physical torture.

(December 1967, from the book *Joni*)

Decades have passed since I experienced that horrible anguish, and the distance was great between 1967 and the summer of 1991. But three weeks of lying still, staring at the ceiling and fighting back tears brought back echoes of that same anguish. Oh, how I longed to be healed of the sores and free from the confines of bed.

The next morning, after Ken left for work, my girlfriend arrived to give me a bath, breakfast, and new dressings on my wounds. Before she went to the kitchen to pour coffee, she flicked on the little TV by my dresser and tuned in *The Today Show*. I was relieved she had left the room, which meant I didn't have to relate or force a smile. I was still down, very down.

After the news, the interviewer, Bryant Gumbel, introduced the next segment. A shot of Derek Humphry, sitting relaxed and comfortable on the set, flashed on the screen. I recognized him from my years of advocacy work in the disability community. He was president of the Hemlock Society, an organization that promotes the idea that terminally ill people should have the legal right to choose the timing of their own death.

Bryant held up Mr. Humphry's book, *Final Exit*.

He tilted it and read the subtitle: The Practicalities of Self-Deliverance and Assisted Suicide for the Dying. Even though I had been out of commission and in bed for weeks, I had heard about *Final Exit*. Some called it controversial, others said it should never have been published, still others insisted bookstores should boycott it. Bryant put down the book and asked, "No qualms about the possibility that this book could get into the hands of someone who is simply depressed but very curable?"

Mr. Humphry argued dispassionately, almost serenely, that he was not promoting suicide, but that dying individuals who wish to achieve a painless death ought to be allowed to plan for it. From his point of view, that meant a person should study suicide options, including different kinds of pills and their dosage, self-starvation, and the implications an act of suicide might have on an insurance policy.

My girlfriend came back into the room and shifted my body closer to the edge of the bed to begin exercising my legs. As she mechanically pushed my paralyzed legs through range-of-motion exercises, I remained riveted to the television.

The interviewer turned from Mr. Humphry and introduced Dr. Robert McAfee, a surgeon from the American Medical Association. Bryant posed a frank and open question, the very one I was thinking. "Do you regret the fact that this book is on sale?"

The doctor shifted in his seat, looking a little

uncomfortable. The response he gave touched on the problems every physician faces when his patient is near death. No doctor enjoys seeing someone under his care suffer through pain. And although pain management has advanced considerably, some patients can't face physical discomfort as well as others. It's a tough and perplexing situation for all concerned.

The doctor concluded, "When there's a situation of significant suffering, then appropriate medication to control pain, to hasten the end . . . may occur."

Bryant looked perplexed. The doctor's response did not at all run crossgrain to the premise of the book on suicide. "So what's the difference?"

Dr. McAfee added that a doctor shouldn't do anything illegal. At that point I was as confused as the interviewer. Was "hastening the end" of a terminally ill person okay as long as it wasn't illegal?

After a minute or two, the mini-debate between the author of *Final Exit* and the doctor from the AMA fizzled. Bryant shrugged his shoulders and said, "Gentlemen, I don't think we have so much disagreement as we do varying viewpoints." The camera flashed to the face of the doctor. He nodded and agreed.[1]

No disagreement? Just varying viewpoints?

Did the three men understand what they had just done? Or said? Or suggested to someone like me? As *The Today Show* rambled to the next segment, I fixed my gaze on my lifeless legs being stretched this way and that. Another hour of a tiresome routine. Each morning the same, day in and day out, year after year. At best, boring. At worst, especially on days like this, depressing.

My mind began to play more games. *Since this television show brought up the subject, wouldn't it be nice to let go, give in? You've earned your Brownie points in that wheelchair, and heaven has got to be better than this. When you're back up in your chair, all it will take will be a quick jerk of the steering mechanism on your handicap van, and you'll be over the side of the freeway. Nobody would even know that you committed suicide, and you'll be free of that paralyzed body.*

I shivered and shook the thought out of my head. Yet I couldn't escape the cool, calm rationale of Mr. Humphry telling me in his relaxed tone that certain people in certain circumstances should end it all.

After my girlfriend finished giving me a bath and turned me on my side, I continued the battle with my thoughts. There I was, a woman of faith, experienced in accepting the challenges of a severe disability, basically very content, joyful and peaceful when up and about in my wheelchair. There I was, toying with crazy, suicidal thoughts!

And if I could be tempted, what about the millions of others who watched that interview this morning? And not just depressed disabled people, but anyone with the Monday morning blues. The three professionals on television may have agreed in a detached way that the disagreement over a person's right to choose their own death was a matter of semantics, but my anguished thoughts said otherwise. I was convinced that mine was not the only struggle. There were countless others who were teetering on the implications of Mr. Humphry's words, ready to stumble over "semantics" and take the final exit.

In fact, not long after that interview on television, I was flipping through *Time* magazine and came to a photo that grabbed my attention—a mother staring vacantly, embracing a framed picture of her son. The article was about the mother's anger over the suicide of her clinically depressed son. He had purchased *Final Exit*, following to a T the directives in the book. His family's words were chilling: "He became obsessed with the book. It showed him the way."[2]

I cut the article out of the magazine to save it as a reminder. Obviously a lot of other people, some depressed much more than me, watched the same program.

Varying Viewpoints?

A month later my pressure sores finally closed, and at long last, I was able to get out of bed and sit up in my wheelchair. I was hardly the same woman, no longer thinking morbid thoughts. I was amazingly lighthearted and peaceful. How quickly my depression had disappeared!

But I still couldn't get *The Today Show* segment

off my mind. It was that thing about "varying viewpoints." The words the author and the doctor used in the interview kept sticking with me. One no longer commits suicide, one performs self-deliverance. A physician under a right-to-die law would not give a lethal injection, he would administer an aid-in-dying measure. One would not kill another, one would practice passive/active euthanasia. The phrases themselves seemed as cool and detached as Mr. Humphry.

Why the semantic gymnastics? Why the subtle attempt to clap respectability and sterility around a cold, hard reality? Perhaps proponents of Mr. Humphry's views believe it is necessary to separate the idea of "self-deliverance" from suicide, or "aid in dying" from killing because such actions, at least for the moment, are still considered socially objectionable. Maybe they feel it's better to drain the horror from certain words.

And another thing troubled me. The whole tone of discussion was drained of horror. Isn't dying at the hand of another something that should ignite passion? The dry discourse I saw on television lessened the debate to an anesthetized conversation about varying viewpoints. It made me wonder if somewhere professionals are sitting around open dictionaries trying to invent more euphemisms like "aid-in-dying measure" or "self-deliverance." And if they are, is their motive really to dismantle the long-held ethics that have guided people for centuries?

Maybe yes, maybe no. But this is for certain: Words have power to persuade. One of Mr. Humphry's colleagues had said, "If we try to foist our ideas too strongly and too soon on a society not yet ready to consider them, we will damage our effectiveness. By moving cautiously . . . we gain a larger audience for our views."[3] Is that why the public no longer thinks it's such a terrible idea when a severely disabled or terminally ill person makes a "perfectly reasonable choice" by deciding to end his life?

The whole strategy sounded so tidy, so untainted. But it gave me goosebumps. My mind again raced back to 1967 when I was one of those severely disabled people confined to a hospital room and surrounded by machines and tubes. I know now that my funereal despair was clouded by severe depression. And I also know that I, or my friends and family, might have been open to listening to aid-in-dying suggestions had we been conditioned by pleasant-sounding persuasion.

"Such a shame, so unfortunate. She'd be better off if she'd never made it," one of my distant relatives had sighed. And it almost sounded not half-bad. When you can't think beyond four bleak hospital walls, the words of experts and professionals, even distant relatives, can sound plausible.

So I have to wonder. What *would* I have done had *Final Exit* sat on the shelves of my hospital library?

Two People ... Two Viewpoints

In the following weeks I was back at work writing articles, researching disability documents, telephoning fellow advocates, and doing radio interviews. I collected so many *Time* magazine articles, clippings from *Newsweek*, and cuttings from newspapers, they were spilling off my desk. My co-workers thought I was a bit compulsive, but I was curious to see how others were responding to the new book on suicide on the shelves.

One morning when I arrived at work, I noticed my secretary had placed the latest edition of *Newsweek* on my desk. I studied the title on the cover, "Choosing Death: A How-to Guide to Suicide Stirs Up a Storm." And another subtitle, "More Doctors Are Helping the Very Sick Die Gently."

Immediately I thought of my friend Bob Ball, a business executive who, until last year, served as vice president of a large media corporation. But Lou Gehrig's disease changed all that. The last time I saw him, he was sitting in a wheelchair. But in recent days his disease had intruded further, and now Bob can no longer swallow food. He has a feeding tube. Next will be a respirator. Some would look at Bob, shake their heads, and assign him to the bottom rung of what they call the quality-of-life ladder. I sighed and fixed my gaze on the cover subtitle about doctors helping the very sick die gently.

I flipped open the magazine and read a few of the

articles. The cover title was right; a storm was stirring. "Thou shalt not murder" may have been news 3500 years ago, but not anymore—the right to die had a permanent grip on the public's interest. And the arguments in the articles sounded convincing and compassionate. Who wouldn't want to help the very sick die gently?

I closed the magazine and looked out the window, thinking more about Bob Ball. I pictured him living what's left of his life with courage . . . desperate for breath, yet uncomplaining . . . unable to swallow food, but oddly peaceful . . . only communicating with his eyes and his indomitable smile, yet communicating so much. I pictured his friends and family helping him squeeze every ounce of living out of his days. They took several hours recently to load him into a handicap van for a drive to the beach. On one hand I knew what he and his family would say about a book on methods of suicide. But on the other hand, I knew Bob would want his soon-coming death to be gentle, serene, dignified.

I opened the *Newsweek* once again. I reread the stories of other people whose problems were as insidious as Lou Gehrig's disease. The story of one woman named Helen touched me deeply. After her husband committed suicide, sixty-two-year-old Helen worked three jobs to support her children and hold onto her home. But a serious heart problem changed everything. In between many operations she remained a model patient at the rehab center, cheering her roommates, and chatting with visitors long after she should have been resting.

Even when one operation forced her onto a ventilator, Helen never withdrew from life, delighting in the nurses who fixed her hair and fussed over her makeup. Her spirits remained strong even though her body continued to weaken. Next was the amputation of a leg. Then the other leg. Then Helen changed—it was as though someone robbed all her joy. One afternoon she beckoned to a nurse to read her lips and write down a note. "I have decided to end my life as I do not want to live like this. I don't want to make a big deal of this."[4]

The respirator was removed. It took a little more than a week for her wish to be granted.

Helen's problems were as critical as Bob's, but she held quite a different opinion of her debilitating condition. Helen hated her life. Semantics and varying viewpoints were of little use to her. She could have cared less that an aid-in-dying measure was socially objectionable. The hard, cold reality of her impending death was beyond debate. She despised ethical discussion about her situation. "I don't want to live like this" was her matter-of-fact, no-nonsense last will and testament.

As I studied her photo in the magazine, I felt I could read her thoughts. Thoughts that were all too familiar, frightening feelings I had wrestled with just weeks earlier. *I am tired, just plain worn out from living life with hands that don't work and feet that don't walk. I'm not pitying poor me, I'm just weary and ready to let go.*

"Oh God, where has this high-tech world brought us," I whispered as I pushed aside the news magazine. "I see Bob's point of view and also ... Helen's."

2

The Pain Is Real

There it was at the top of the *New York Times* bestseller list, Derek Humphry's *Final Exit*. How could one nine-minute interview on a morning television program send thousands of readers to flood the bookstores?

For weeks the story captured the headlines. Cameras zoomed in on every appearance made by Derek Humphry. Microphones picked up every statement. But the famous author of a best-selling book wasn't the only one making headlines.

Growing Support of the "Right to Die" a Worrisome Trend

What's All the Fuss About Tube Feeding?

The Disabled Demand Rights and Choices

Christian Disabled Unite Against Assisted Suicide

I wondered about the families standing behind the bold type. I recalled the newspaper banners blaring out the names of people like Karen Quinlan, a young, active woman who, in the early '70s, became brain injured and linked to a life-support system. Televised images of her grieving parents flashed across the evening news. In the '80s the Quinlans became household words along with the parents of Nancy Cruzan and Christine Busalacchi, other young women in semi-comatose states. Reporters and cameramen with lights and microphones rushed at these weary families as they exited hospitals and courthouses. Advocacy groups from both positions filed court briefs and circulated petitions. The parents' attempts to remove their loved one's life support systems became the center ring of a media circus.

But famous families of suffering people were not the only ones in the headlines. Their doctors even stepped into the center stage of the nightly news.

Like in the story of Janet Adkins. When Janet learned she had Alzheimer's disease, she felt she could not face the humiliation of an encroaching disability. She showed few symptoms of Alzheimer's, but that didn't quell terrifying thoughts. *What will happen to me? How will I survive? Who will feed me when I cannot feed myself? How can I bear being dependent on others?* Janet captured her fears in a note, "I have Alzheimer's disease and I do not want it to progress any further. I don't choose to put my family or myself through the agony of this terrible disease."[1]

But Janet was not about to expose her pain to the glare of the media. So after making quiet, private arrangements, she flew across country to Michigan, rented a car, drove up to a rusting Volkswagen van in a park, stepped inside, and allowed Dr. Jack Kevorkian, a retired pathologist, to hook her up to a contraption that would cause her own death. When she touched a button, an IV dripped into her veins one drug that put her to sleep, and another drug that then stopped her heart.

Moments after Dr. Kevorkian notified police, the media focused on the incident. Articles about the "death doctor" appeared in every major magazine. Once again, headlines shouted.

Outspoken Doctor Takes the Case
for Euthanasia to the Public

"Suicide Machine" Smokes Out
Hippocratic Hypocrites

She's Got Her Wish, Says Dr. Jack Kevorkian

The retired pathologist continued to stay in the media light. He helped two more disabled women commit suicide the following year. Sherry, with multiple sclerosis, and Marjorie, with a pelvic disease. And he didn't stop there.

More front-page coverage accompanied the deaths of Sherry and Marjorie. There were special investigative reports. Articles of in-depth analysis. Probing editorials. Virtually overnight the public was drawn into a hot debate over a person's right to die. Advocacy groups to the right and left nailed the doctor against the ethical wall, sparking a new round of discussions about death and dying among ethicists and activists on both sides of the issue. Every time I traveled to Washington, D.C., I encountered advocacy friends who slammed their fists against their wheelchairs, saying, "Something's got to be done!"

Yet, many families that included either a disabled, dying, or even elderly member remained quiet during the outrage. Many people with debilitating diseases themselves fell silent and merely watched the debate from a distance. Some viewed the doctor as a lone and sympathetic compatriot, someone on their side who understood. Obviously the decisions of Janet, Sherry, and Marjorie touched a fragile and painful nerve.

Helpful Information

Janet and those like her made headlines because of the bizarre circumstances surrounding their deaths. The Cruzans and families like them captured the spotlight because the courts got involved after hospitals refused to comply with the families' requests to have respirators disconnected or feeding tubes withdrawn.

But these people are the exceptions.

The vast majority of suicides of elderly, terminally ill, or even disabled persons occurs quietly within homes and institutions, far from the media, the courts, and the eye of the public. These are hurting, hopeless people who never make the nightly news. These are the ones living a quiet desperation: The woman with cancer, seesawing in and out of remission. The young boy in a semi-coma, making eye contact, half smiling, and then drifting away again. The carpenter who broke his neck falling from a second-story window and now, abandoned by his wife, living in a nursing home.

Some are terminally ill but not imminently dying.

Some are elderly and have entered the process of dying.

Some are in a semi-coma.

Some are suspended in a persistent vegetative state.

Some are not dying at all. They are just plain depressed because of a mental, emotional, or physical disability. And many are the mothers, fathers, sisters, and brothers of these hurting people.

They would squirm in a spotlight. Probably just a few close relatives or neighbors are aware of their desperation. They feel alone and very lonely, afraid to draw too many curious onlookers into their circle of pain. But occasionally they or their families feel compelled to write about their journey of heartache and anguish. And a few of them write to me.

Dear Joni,

I've heard you mention a booklet titled "Is God Really in Control?" I would appreciate getting a copy of this booklet as I am struggling with that very issue.

My sister Janet, who is 23, was in a serious car accident. She had very critical lung and brain stem damage, and now, four months later, she is still in a coma, mostly unresponsive to life around her. She had a good life with friends, church, a straight-A student, a job as a physical therapist; now it all seems wasted.

If she had lost all her physical capabilities, but still retained her mental ability, I could have accepted it so much easier. I'm really struggling with how God could possibly be glorified through this situation. To be honest, it is like a living death—the grief process doesn't end because Janet is still "living." . . . I would please appreciate any helpful information you can send.

Joyce Hutt

I can imagine Joyce sitting vigil by the shadowy bedside of her sister, wondering, waiting, and hoping. But her letter captures something far more poignant. She poses an unspoken question: When, if ever, is life not worth living?

Why is it an unspeakable question? Well, Joyce's brain-injured sister is unable to speak for herself. And who would dare make such a judgment call, especially on behalf of a close friend or family member? Joyce writes that she is looking to God, struggling with God. She doesn't want to *play* God by the guardrail of her sister's hospital bed, arbitrarily ruling that, yes, Janet should die or, no, Janet should live. Who has the right to say whether or not the life of another is worth living? Perhaps a few families like the Cruzans or the Quinlans can bring themselves to openly ask the question and then act on the answer, but thousands like Joyce stand bewildered and confused.

My heart is gripped by her letter. Joyce has poured out personal and terrifying thoughts to me, a person she hasn't even met. And tears filled my eyes when I read her last sentence: "I would please appreciate any helpful information you can send."

It's clear that Joyce and millions like her don't want to make "tragic moral choices." Instead, they want to know what is the right thing to do. They may not know how to phrase it, but they desire to understand the difference between prolonging death and sustaining life. Or for that matter, is there a difference?

How can I best help my family member who is terminally ill? Or elderly? Or dealing with a debilitating disease? Is it ever ethical or appropriate to disconnect someone's life-support systems? If a loved one is dying, can't we just let him die? Please tell me: Is there a difference between withholding medication and disconnecting feeding tubes or IVs? Show me what to do. Tell me what to say. A tidy list of five easy-to-understand steps. Please, a neat conclusion to a painful situation. Yes, please give me helpful information.

What *if* I approached Joyce at her sister's bedside and handed her a nicely typed list of do's and don'ts? Would that give her the tools she really needed?

What's more, what if her sister awoke from the coma just long enough to speak her wishes? She might want to live . . . she might want to die. She might react like the young man in the following letter:

> Dear Joni,
>
> My brother was involved in a motorcycle accident three years ago, which left him a paraplegic. He has never been able to accept his condition. He has been destroying himself ever since. He has terrible bed sores, he has had surgery twice now, he has to stay in bed all the time. They had to take the hip bone, leg and knee bone on one leg, and amputate above the knee on the other. This is due to neglect. He wants to die and he's killing himself slowly.
>
> He is 32 years old—he has such a sharp mind and this is such a waste. The whole family cannot reach him, we are totally frustrated. Any information you could advise would be so appreciated.
>
> > Sincerely,
> >
> > Kathy Bennett

Kathy's brother has weighed his suffering and determined that life is not worth the bother. He holds fast to the right to abuse his body and thereby cause his death.

What do I put in the mail to Kathy's brother? A letter? Books? The name of a local counselor who runs a suicide-prevention program? I just can't allow the letter to go unanswered. Yet I know it's nearly impossible to sit down with someone like this paraplegic to try to argue with reason and objectivity a case for "life worth living." I've read the professional handbooks of counselors, and they all say the same: A person's desire to commit suicide transcends reasoned argument.

So what good would ten objective arguments against suicide do to sway this young man's conviction for self-destruction? I could tell him about my own times of depression, but I'm not the one facing severe amputations. I'm no longer struggling in severe depression; I see things more clearly now, more objectively. But what does that matter to him? A huge chasm lies between his topsy-turvy emotions and my right-side-up reasoning, his frayed feelings and my coolheaded statements, his insensibilities and my sensibilities.

True, people ready to check out of life, like Kathy's brother, can occasionally be talked down off the ledge. But many times the rational appeals don't reach their target.

Helpful Information Isn't Enough

This lesson was driven home through my old friend, Ada Walker. Ada was my hospital roommate when I was first injured, and for over a year she and I shared a six-bed ward with several other girls. Ada and I were a lot alike: We were young, we were both in accidents, we were left quadriplegic, and we hated being handicapped. We shared our pain, our bitterness, our horrible fear of what would happen next, who would feed us, how could we bear being dependent on others. Misery loved company back then, and Ada and I would spend long hours commiserating over cold hospital food and dirty sheets.

But that's where the similarities ended. Over the long months of hospitalization, I noticed a change in Ada. Whenever I wheeled past her bed on my way to physical therapy, I observed the difference:

Ada had given up. I was still fighting.

Ada had quit. I was steaming mad.

Ada had glazed eyes. Mine were ablaze with angry fire.

Ada had stopped going to therapy. I went and worked hard just to prove to those jerky doctors that they didn't know what they were talking about because I was going to walk.

Ada saw no way out. I was ready to bust out the front door of the hospital.

Ada sullenly shrugged her shoulders at God. I was ready to punch God in the nose.

Her roommates and I were troubled that Ada, during those long reclusive hours, was obviously maneuvering a deliberate and methodical suicide. Nuts! If I were to end it all, I would have careened off a high curb in a fit of explosive anger.

The numb, lifeless pall hanging over her bed told me she would give anything for pills or a razor. At that point I was not facing the same suicidal despair. For the moment, anger fueled my energy to face each day and suicide, as far as I was concerned, would have been a cop-out. Nobody had to convince me of the ethical, right, and appropriate action—it was to break out of that stinking hospital!

By the way, there was one more striking difference between Ada and me. Ada smoked like a chimney. I didn't. I paused by her bed one day—she was puffing on a cigarette that was stuck in a little tray attached to a long tube, the end of which she clenched between her teeth. She inhaled the smoke deeply, as if to split the seams of her lungs. Then exhaling slowly, Ada would wait a few seconds and suck in the smoke again. "You're going to kill yourself with those things," I said, more than a little concerned.

Ada slowly blew out the smoke and watched it rise. ".Can't wait," she coolly replied.

"Ada, you can't be serious. Hey, we're not going to let you take the easy way out," I said, half joking, looking at our roommates.

Stony silence.

"Look," I said, wheeling closer to her bedside. "Your parents would really take it hard."

She turned her head on the pillow and puffed further on her cigarette.

My friend, in spite of my best efforts to dispense helpful information, had made the judgment call. My feeble efforts at being objective fell flat. Life, Ada dispassionately believed, was not worth living. Years later a lung infection sealed her decision.

Ada's story is bittersweet. Bitter in that she, like Kathy's brother, purposefully abused her body in order to engineer an early death. Sweet in that perhaps a year or so before her death, Ada finally crossed that huge chasm between despair and hope and found life worth living. In that final year she crossed the unbridgeable gulf from hopelessness to hope. Her topsy-turvy emotions turned right side up.

Whenever I returned to the hospital for a checkup, I always made certain to spend time with Ada. I'd sit across from her, amazed. She had become one of the most buoyant, lively people I knew, inspiring and encouraging all of her old roommates, and everyone else from the janitor to nursing supervisors.

But her spirit could not overrule damage done to her body. Not even new hope was able to short-circuit the death fuse she had ignited years earlier.

For Ada, even if information would have helped, it arrived too late.

3

Why Not Die?

My desk couldn't contain any more articles or clippings, so I opened up a file folder, shoved everything in, and stuck it on a shelf. The question all those articles raised, however, was not about to quietly sit on a shelf.

When is it right to die?

Thousands like Ada Walker found what they believed to be the permanent answer. "Disabled people all over the country have killed themselves," according to the World Institute on Disability. "... they see no hope, no future."[1]

Is that the answer? Is it right to die when people see no hope, no future? Is it right to die when the pain becomes excessive, the medical costs prohibitive, the personal dignity shattered? Where is the line drawn? And who has the right to draw it? When is it right to say, "This much I can take, and no more!"

Staring down at my paralyzed legs to contemplate those questions, I noticed on the floor the surge suppressor with six electrical outlets. One plug for my computer. Another for the printer. Another for the cassette player. Another plug for the little space heater. This much it takes and no more. I don't dare plug any other equipment into that suppressor or else I blow a fuse and out goes the power in my office.

Some people are like that. A terminal illness. Add to that chemotherapy. Then add radiation treatments. Then another surgery. Perhaps another. More treatment. And then something snaps. All their strength drains and they simply can't take any more.

Is that how it goes? Does each of us have the right to choose the timing of our own death depending on our tolerance for either pain, expense, or indignity? Of this much I was certain: There is for each of us a time to die, and when that time comes, we should be prepared to go. But the problem remains: Exactly when is it time?

When Is It Right to Die? It's None of Your Business

"You want a time? I'll give you a time," I could almost hear Arlene say. "It's when *you* decide. Period."

Arlene Randolph was athletic and full of life, but a fall during a hiking trip in the coastal mountains of California damaged her spinal cord. She became severely paralyzed. Doctors kept telling her that her life would brighten as soon as she could learn to sit up . . . as soon as she could get a better wheelchair

. . . as soon as she could have a special-order bed . . . as soon as she could go home. Life for Arlene didn't happen that neatly or cleanly. As her husband Phil put it, "Everything that could go wrong went wrong for her."

A self-directed young woman, Arlene knew whose life it was—her own. It wasn't her husband's and it wasn't her two children's. Her life was not owned by the doctors and nurses she left behind at the hospital. And the life-and-death choices she was contemplating certainly weren't the business of her rabbi or even the pastor who ran the little support group in her community.

Less than a year into her disability, Arlene made a decision. Unwilling to face a life without hands that worked or feet that walked, she decided to starve herself to death. Her husband stood with her and her decision. "She was set in her ways and that's the way she's always been. And she was not depressed," her husband said.

I knew Arlene's disability was not a terminal illness, and she was far from death's door. She was, like me, disabled and her decision was a deliberate suicide. Knowing about the physical pain that accompanies starvation, I sent her a letter. "Maybe our situations aren't exactly the same," I wrote, "but I can understand the loneliness, the confusion, the battle with resentment, and the many questions." As a fellow disabled person, I pleaded with her to reconsider. But Arlene died not long after she received my letter.

I talked with Phil on the phone after his wife's death. "Do you wish Arlene would have waited a little longer before she decided to kill herself?"

There was silence on the other end and then a tentative "Yes. Yes. I think about it all the time." Then Phil was quick to add, "But it wasn't my choice to stop her. In fact, all of us, the whole family, supported her."

Arlene's death was her own business. That's what she believed. And even though pain management and provisions for independent living are better than ever for disabled people, things like customized wheelchairs, special-order beds, attendant care, adapted home environments, and financial aid are, to some people, the trees. The forest is that they just don't want to live with a severe handicapping condition, and they believe the decision to die belongs to them alone.

I can't help but picture Arlene's life before her accident. It's easy to imagine her climbing the cliffs of Big Sur, blazing a trail into the wilderness, or powering ahead on her bicycle, leaving the pack in the dust. And in a way her choice to die fits her do-it-yourself profile. After all, Arlene was obviously a first-class individual, a born and bred American who gripped onto her individualism as a highly prized value. Her brand of private initiative found its logical and ultimate expression in her decision to die. What's ironic is that in our society, which regards individualism as a valued tradition, Arlene's choice seems common, acceptable, and not surprising.

But was Arlene's demise her business and hers alone? To make a decision before life involuntarily leaves us is a decision we have the power to make. But is it possible such a choice is the ultimate expression of selfishness?

When Is It Right to Die?
When It's Too Expensive to Live

"Hey! For a lot of people death is just plain cheaper than life!"

I never would have dreamed that would be the question on the minds of most people at a banquet attended by Christian health-care professionals. I was invited to present the main address and the topic was "Assisted Suicide in the Disability Community." During the question and answer time, the concern turned to rising health-care costs. One doctor shook his head and said, "Costs for treatment are soaring beyond what anyone can handle. People are running up bills not covered by insurance or Medicare." He tapped his fingers on the table and added, "I think this whole life-and-death debate is going to be settled by economics."

I shivered. I couldn't help but think of the grandmother in a nursing home deciding to refuse treatment because her $10,000 a month care is eroding the college savings of her grandchildren. And I thought of the subtle pressure that society places on dying, terminally ill, or debilitated people, reminding them that expensive treatment does, after all, have its limits.

Are we to the point where health-care costs have forced us to put a different price tag on each person's life? What about those most economically vulnerable? A decision to forego treatment and face a quick death may be one of a few options for wealthy or well-insured persons, but a decision to cut life short may be the *only* option for people who are poor, abandoned, or severely debilitated.

When Is It Right to Die?
When Death Is Easier than Facing Life

"There's a time when life is the foe and death is the friend."

A black mustache and beard. A black shirt. Black trousers, shoes, and socks. That was the first thing I noticed about Ken Bergstedt when his father wheeled him into my office. But our conversation was surprisingly lighthearted. While his father sat on the office sofa, Ken and I gabbed about our disabilities, how irked we were at wheelchair manufacturers that kept hiking prices, and how it was a good idea to always double-rinse the sheepskins we slept on. Our hour appointment passed quickly. Ken and his dad returned to their RV, and a day later headed back to their home in Las Vegas, Nevada.

After Ken left, I mused over our similarities and differences. We were old veterans when it came to our disabilities, but we were quite different when it came to our faith. My limitations had forged a stronger faith. His limitations had drained him of any spiritual notions. But I was grateful he kept in touch. I received a letter a couple of months later in which Ken included a few photos of how his dad modified their RV vehicle for his wheelchair.

A year later I read about Ken in the newspaper. The article was cut-and-dried, explaining that Kenneth Bergstedt, a ventilator-dependent Nevada man, now wished his father to assist him in suicide. Ken's decision was exacerbated by the fear that his dad would soon pass away due to failing health. Both were afraid that Ken would not be adequately cared for once his dad died.

It was virtually impossible to get through to Ken once the news media got involved. Nevertheless, I tried to contact him, writing, "Is it true you said in an article that you have 'no happy or encouraging expectations to look for from life, and you live with constant fears and apprehensions?' Those words are chilling—they remind me of a time when I said the same. But don't have them pull you off the respirator."

I don't think my letter ever reached him. And from reading further accounts in the newspapers, it was clear why Ken wanted his father to kill him. Life seemed more frightening than death.

Four months later I picked up the morning paper and saw a small notice on the bottom of the front page. Ken had died. His father died, just a short time later.

The prospect of life without the familiarity of his dad's care was unbearable. Death, to Ken, appeared to be more of a friend than the known hell of life. The irony is, life without his father was yet to be lived, it didn't have to be hellish. I personally knew of people in his community who wanted to help him interpret the future as a friend. But Ken refused. What he knew of life appeared more ominous than what he knew of death.

Many would say that Kenneth Bergstedt from Las Vegas, Nevada, took a bigger gamble in choosing a black and uncertain oblivion over the brighter possibilities of life with potential for change.

When Is It Right to Die?
When Death Is a Matter of Mercy

"No decent human being would allow an animal to suffer without putting it out of its misery. It is only to human beings that human beings are so cruel as to allow them to live on in pain, in hopelessness, in living death, without moving a muscle to help them," said Isaac Asimov.[2]

Long ago I went to see a movie with my friends called *They Shoot Horses, Don't They?* I had just been discharged from the rehab center, and my friends thought it would be nice to enjoy some Friday night fun. Besides, the title had "horses" in it, so the movie couldn't be that bad, right?

Wrong. It was a story about a depressed person who wanted a friend to put a gun to her head to relieve her suffering. When the friend protested, Jane Fonda said with woeful eyes, "They shoot horses, don't they?" At that point we left the movie.

Art sometimes imitates life and although the message of that movie may have been shocking when it was released twenty years ago, today more than 63 percent of Americans approve, in certain cases, of mercy killing.[3]

But what induces a person to cause a death and say, "This is for your own good"? Is it indeed because pain is excessive? Pain management is the most sophisticated and advanced as it's ever been. Is it living with limitations? Who knows what Arlene would have decided had she given her wheelchair a chance. Is it a suffering loved one's shattered dignity and loss of hope? Ah, are we motivated to mercy kill because the loved one is hurting, or are we motivated by a confused sense of guilt and sympathy, suffering as we watch him?

"No decent human being would allow an animal to suffer without putting it out of its misery," said Mr. Asimov. Oddly, suffering animals aren't endowed with human characteristics such as dignity or hope, no matter how forcibly Isaac Asimov or moviemakers may argue.

Mercy is defined as "kind or compassionate treatment."[4] Mr. Asimov chides people for not moving a muscle to help those who hurt. I heartily agree. But are there not better ways to demonstrate kindness and compassion other than to send a loved one off into a black and uncertain oblivion?

Defining the Right to Die

Just listen to a few people respond to the question "When is it right to die?" and you'll hear a mixed muddle of not only when but who wants to die, how, and why! In the examples above, no one was actually dying. Yet whether the person is dying, debilitated, terminally ill, or the family member of one of these, all use the same language and similar arguments. In order to clear up the confusion, let's look at a few terms.

Euthanasia is supposed to signify "good death," but today's meaning of the word is confusing because it conjures up images of everything from pulling the plug on a dying loved one to the killing of millions in Nazi Germany who were considered socially unuseful. Practically speaking, euthanasia means to produce death or assist an individual in achieving death because others, or even the patient himself, considers life no longer worth living. The motive is usually to relieve suffering, save money, or do away with the indignities associated with dying. Under this broad definition fall a few more specific terms.

Voluntary euthanasia is to cause death with the person's approval and consent.

Nonvoluntary euthanasia is to cause death without a person's consent through approval secured from a family member, hospital panel, or court. The key is that the patient is incompetent, and someone else must decide either what the patient would have wanted or what is in his best interests.

Involuntary euthanasia is to cause the death of a person against his will under whatever circumstances.

Death selection involves systematic involuntary euthanasia against the lives of people no longer considered socially useful. This type of euthanasia threatens a wide range of people, including the elderly, the habitually criminal, the mentally ill, or the disabled. Currently there are no groups officially proposing death selection, but population control and cost containment are two primary arguments used when the subject is debated.

Active euthanasia is mercy kiliing by which a person takes action to cause someone's death.

Passive euthanasia is mercy killing by withholding or withdrawing medical treatment or food and water.

Assisted suicide is when a physician or family member aids a person toward death.

Death with dignity is a phrase that tries to say one thing but means another. After all, death is the final indignity of losing all that one commands in life. Death remains, in the words from the Bible, the last enemy. People may die serenely or peaceably, but with dignity? Modern usage of the phrase implies that death by suicide or homicide is inherently preferable to death by natural causes. Euthanasia proponents explain that death with dignity means allowing a person to die free from the dehumanization and pain often brought about by the application of extraordinary medical efforts.

Currently there are no laws that require that a dying person be kept alive by heroic measures. Also, all mentally competent persons have the legal right to refuse medical treatment provided they have received sufficient information from the physician to make an informed consent.[5]

Right to die is another phrase that is trying to say one thing but means another. Taken literally, "right to die" is senseless. There's no such thing as a right to something unavoidable and inevitable. But in common usage the phrase sometimes means the "right to be allowed to die" from a terminal illness, and at other times, a supposed "right to be killed."

Former Surgeon General C. Everett Koop explains euthanasia and the right to die using one word.

> The whole thing about euthanasia comes down to one word: motive. If your motive is to alleviate suffering while a patient is going through the throes of dying, and you are using medication that alleviates suffering, even though it might shorten his life by a few hours, that is not euthanasia. But if you are giving him a drug intended to shorten his life, then your motivation is for euthanasia. . . .[6]

Quality of life is a phrase of recent phenomenon. Fifty years ago people who broke their necks like me died—no need to worry about quality of life when you're dead.

Today it's a different story. Within the last few decades, medical technology has given us high-tech helps to improve a person's so-called quality of life. And this has granted society the power to control whether a person lives or dies, all depending on the application of a few technological gizmos or new-fangled drugs. A respirator enables a polio quadri-plegic like my friend Lily to breathe. A sophisti-cated drug stabilizes the emotions of my neighbor Linda, who struggles with a manic-depression disor-der. Or even an indwelling catheter keeps the urinary plumbing of someone like me flowing.

Kidney machines, pacemakers, insulin injections, and even medication to manage either pain or depression—all of these things, to one degree or another, increase one's "quality of life."

However, by virtue of those high-tech gizmos or drug therapies, people's lives begin to be defined by whether or not they can function. Lily, thanks to a respirator, is able to sit up in a wheelchair and go about life as a "normal" person. People like Linda in pain or depression can, with medication, hold down a job and raise a family. They can function and thus society moves them up a few notches on its so-called quality-of-life scale, a few notches above others less able such as my friend Bob, who is rapidly deteriorating from Lou Gehrig's disease and can only lie in bed and blink his eyes.

Some say that a society that measures people in terms of their quality of life will preserve those who have a potential to function . . . and neglect those who don't. Oddly enough, society will ascribe to physically fit and intellectually capable people a very high quality of life, despite the fact that they are sometimes the most miserable. Yet society will ascribe a very low quality of life to poor, debilitated people, despite the fact that they are sometimes the most content.

"Quality of life" is a phrase that is generally used as a counterbalance to the term sanctity of life. Which brings me to the next term.

Absolute value reflects the long-held ethic that human life holds complete worth without relationship to other factors, including a person's functioning ability. In other words, no matter how incapacitated Bob becomes from Lou Gehrig's disease, his life will never lose value.

Relative value is what people ascribe to human life when it is appraised in relation to other factors such as how much a person can or cannot do. By this definition the value and meaning of Bob's life is related to how incapacitated he becomes.

Life, from varying viewpoints, has either absolute or relative value. Which is it? And how do those varying viewpoints have a bearing on preserving or rejecting the life of a warm-blooded, breathing human being named Bob, who lies flat and face-up on the bottom rung of society's quality-of-life ladder?

People's Viewpoints ... Society's Trends

When. Who. What. How. Why. You know the issue is confusing when you have to get so nitpicky about definitions. And although dictionary terms make the life-and-death struggle sound neat and clean, it is not. As I said, death is the great indignity, the last enemy, and we should be shocked by the stories of people like Arlene and Ken. But why aren't we?

Euthanasia is not uncommon. It has been closeted in hospital ethics committees as death certificates are divvied out, and cloaked in back rooms of maternity wards where severely handicapped infants have been left to starve to death.

On one hand it's good to yank euthanasia out of the closet and expose it to the open air of public debate because people need to understand and be able to make informed decisions. On the other hand, the sheer repetition of stories like Arlene's and Ken's gradually dulls the shock effect. No longer is the public outraged by the starvation of handicapped infants in hospital wards or the gun held to the head of the person with Alzheimer's disease. Instead, people begin to argue for positions to moderate extremes, such as the Dr. Kevorkian types, or even euthanasia involving the extremes of bullets, plastic bags, or pillows smashed over faces. Or perhaps they accept the premise of euthanasia and only challenge the means to achieve it: "Keep euthanasia safe and clean in the hospital wards where it belongs."

And gradually, though no one remembers exactly how it happened, the unthinkable becomes tolerable. And then acceptable. And then legal. And then applaudable.

At this stage of the debate, confusion still reigns. And in a way, I am glad. The battle is still being waged, the questions and answers are still being sorted out, and we have not yet come to the point where society grants carte blanche approval to people like Arlene and Ken and others who wish to secure either legal or unlawful help to euthanize themselves. At this stage no state in our nation and no country of the world has voted a law onto the books legalizing voluntary or nonvoluntary euthanasia. No religion supports it and every physicians' oath condemns it. For centuries civilized countries, through law and religion, have safeguarded life, especially the lives of those most weak and vulnerable. And what an irony that euthanasia has suddenly become popular at a time when our resources are infinitely greater than they were in the days when mercy killing was unheard of.

But there is now a pull on people's minds and a passion to exercise rights. There is a push for legislation. There is a rush to clamp control around a rapidly advancing medical technology. There is a race to slap together a structure of ethics to accommodate the morals of euthanasia.

Everybody is coming up with a point of view, and society is rapidly and collectively forming one as well.

Now, what is your point of view?

PART TWO

A Time to Choose

4

Your Decision Matters to Others

For the moment, forget everything you've ever read in either a right-to-die or right-to-life brochure. Put aside the court rulings. Push out of your mind the tug-at-your-heart stories you've read in the newspapers.

Now, with no one reading your thoughts, may I ask: Do you know when it is right to die? For you? For your family? Please, I realize this may not be a theoretical question for you. You may be one who could write a real-life tug-at-your-heart story. And you may have already made up your mind about how and when you want to die. Whatever your response, I want you to know that your decision matters.

It matters more than you realize.

Let me explain. Since I served on a council that drafted major civil rights legislation, my husband Ken, a high school government teacher, asked me to speak to his classes on the subject of legalizing euthanasia. California is the testing ground for various right-to-die initiatives, and Ken wanted me to talk to his students about the implications of a right-to-die law. The classroom was crowded with kids standing along the back wall and leaning against the side chalkboards.

I was surprised by how interested they were as I divulged my despair of earlier days. I admitted my relief that no right-to-die law existed when I was in the hospital and hooked up to machines. I then underscored how critical it was for every student to become informed and involved in shaping society's response to the problem. Then I added, "What role do you think society should play in helping people decide when it is right to die?"

A few hands went up. I could tell by their answers that they felt society should take action to help hurting and dying people, some students insisting on life no matter how burdensome the treatment, and a few wanting to help by hurrying along the death process.

One student shared how his mother was getting demoralized by the burden of taking care of his mentally handicapped sister. He felt society should, in his words, "do something."

"Like what?" I playfully challenged.

"Like . . . I'm not sure, but society ought to get more involved in the lives of people like my mother."

I glanced at Ken. He nodded as if to give the go-ahead to take a free rein with this young man. "May I ask what you have done to get more involved?"

The student smiled and shrugged.

"How have you helped alleviate the burden?

Have you taken your sister on an outing lately? Maybe to the beach?" I teased. "Have you offered to do some shopping for your mother? Maybe your mom wouldn't be so demoralized, wouldn't feel so stressed or burdened if you rolled up your sleeves a little higher to help."

A couple of his friends by the chalkboard laughed and threw wads of paper at him. "Okay, okay, I see your point," he chuckled.

I smiled. "My point is this: Society is not a bunch of people way out there who sit around big tables and think up political trends or cultural drifts. Society is you. Your actions, your decisions matter. What you do or don't do has a rippling effect on everyone around you. And even on a smaller scale, your participation can even make a huge difference in what your family decides to do with your sister."

The classroom fell silent and I knew the lesson was being driven home. I paused, scanned the face of each student and closed, saying, "You, my friends, are society."

Your Point of View Matters

And that's how much your view matters. You may be the one who fiercely advocates pulling the plug, or the one who fights to keep a heart pumping until the bitter end. Whichever, you must in the words of John Donne, know this:

No man is an island entire of itself; every man is a piece of the continent, a part of the main . . . any

man's death diminishes me, because I am involved
in mankind; and therefore never send to know for
whom the bell tolls; it tolls for thee.[1]

We are such private people. We would like to be
able to make a life-and-death decision in a vacuum
or even at an arm's-length distance from others. But
we can't. Your point of view and how you act on it,
let's say as you lie in bed with a terminal illness,
not only matters to you and your family, it matters
to a wide network of friends and associates. In other
words, society. The cultural drift is channeled by
your decision to either pull the plug or hold onto
life.

In fact, will you permit me to get personal? If you
can, dismiss your real-life circumstances for a
moment. Let's pretend you *are* in bed with a
terminal illness, and doctors say you could live for
another six months. Your pain *can* be effectively
managed. And you *do* have an opportunity to make
a choice about prolonging medical treatment. Laws
will permit you to decline that treatment, and your
family says it's up to you. I know it's hard to
pretend such an antiseptic situation, devoid of real
grief and actual anguish, because distress would
play a key role. But given this sterile scenario, what
would you do? What would you say?

Are you one who might say, "It's none of your
business. I'll control how and when I die, and what's
more, I don't care about any poem by John Donne
and I feel no responsibility to society. I'm only
responsible to myself and those I love."

I hear what you're saying. But when people maintain that their death is their own business and that of "those I love," they do not consider the significance of their decision on the wider circle of life. A decision to cut short life, even if only a few months, does not stop with "those I love," but affects a whole network of relationships: friends, former colleagues, teachers, distant family members, casual acquaintances, and even nurses and doctors who occasionally stop by your bedside.

Just what effect might your decision have? Your gutsy choice to face suffering head-on forces others around you to sit up and take notice. It's called strengthening the character of a helping society. When people observe perseverance, endurance, and courage, their moral fiber is reinforced. Conversely, your choice to bow out of life can and does weaken the moral resolve of that same society.

Years after my hospitalization, my mother is still receiving letters from nurses, cafeteria workers, and a family whose brain-damaged daughter was hooked up to machines two beds down from me in the intensive care unit. My parents made gutsy choices that involved facing suffering head-on. And the decisions they made regarding my care have had a lasting impact on these people. And who knows what they one day will decide if faced with life-and-death decisions.

If you believe your decision is private and independent, your choice to speed up the dying process is like playing a delicate game of Pick Up Sticks.

You carefully lift a stick hoping not to disturb the intricate web. But just when you think you've succeeded, your independent action ends up jiggling the fragile balance.

And as it says somewhere in the Bible, "None of us lives to himself alone and none of us dies to himself alone."[2]

You Have Your Rights ... Sort of

"But I have a right to decide what's best for me. I'm entitled to exercise my independence. It's fundamental to what this country is all about. Even the courts recognize my autonomy as a patient."

True, as a mentally competent person, the judge would probably bang the gavel in your favor. Like you said, you have rights and you may end up literally dying for them.

But like all other liberties, your choice is not absolute, no ifs, ands, or buts. Your self-determination to die has strings attached if it adversely affects the rights of others. That's why more than half the states in our country have laws against aiding a person in suicide. Think it through: If everybody ended their lives as a solution to problems, the very fabric of our society would ultimately unravel, and with it all the other individual rights you enjoy.

Yes, you have a glistening right of privacy, as long as it does not overshadow the rights of others. For this reason, legalized euthanasia could seriously infringe on the rights of many physicians. You might want to exercise a right to die, but you cannot ask a physician, whose duty is to heal, to comply with your wishes or to even make a referral. No person, in the name of self-determination, can oblige a doctor to inject him with orphenadrine when it goes against the physician's oath to heal.

But wait, it sounds a little like we're trading baseball cards here.

Like, "My rights are more valuable than yours!"

"Oh, yeah? Well, my one right is worth more than your three combined!"

Our rights are not things that can be exchanged, bargained over, or transferred like property. Essentially, rights are *moral claims* to be recognized by law, not things to be traded.[3] And moral claims have to take into account responsibility, limits on freedom, and ethical standards that reflect the good of the entire community.

When we clamor about the sanctity of our individual rights, we may be reinforcing an all-too-human failing, and that is the tendency to place ourselves at the center of the moral universe. We label our desires "rights" as if to give those willful determinations a showy kind of dignity. If taken to the extreme, radical clamor over individual rights can lead to one indignation after another about the inherent limitations of society, and we will never be satisfied.

As I shared in Ken's government class, "You, my friend, are society." So welcome to the club of community, and even though you may try to drown out other styles of discourse with your shout over personal rights, the community around you may have a thing or two to say, and they may say it a lot louder. After all, community can only progress when its individuals exercise higher moral choices, and community is sacrificed when individuals choose with only themselves in mind.

God's Laws Make for a Better Society and Vice Versa

Are you with me? For the sake of argument, remember our sterile scenario: You're still in that bed with a terminal illness and a choice to make. Yes, I realize it's hard to think about such things as "moral claims" and "the good of society" when you're approaching death's door, but bear with me. Hold on to the guardrail of that hospital bed and let's broaden the scenario a bit.

Picture yourself biding time and glancing occasionally at the television bolted to the ceiling at the foot of your bed. The evening news is on, and the commentator launches into the story at the top of the hour.

"Within days," he announces, "voters will have an opportunity to pass a state initiative that would legally permit a terminally ill patient to request a lethal injection from his doctor."

The news commentator drones on but your mind is already racing. *This is the answer, you think, the answer for thousands of terminally ill people who*

would never buy John Donne's rhetoric or a lot of
sympathetic mush about "the good of society."
Make the right to die legal and everything is taken
care of: No more families going bankrupt because of
outrageous hospital bills, not to mention the burden
to Medicare or insurance companies. And no more
parents biting their nails over what to do with their
daughter in a long, drawn-out coma. Simply make
the right to die legal, and if legislators don't have
the guts to do it, then get it on the state ballot and
let public sentiment pass the law.

Take the scenario even further. You pick up the
phone on your bedside stand, dial a family member,
and tell him to grab your absentee ballot from the
pile of mail on the kitchen table—before you arrive
at death's door, you want to leave an epitaph and
vote yes on this thing!

It sounds good and, like one of my husband's
students, I admire your desire to get involved. But
wait a minute. Let's say the bulk of voters share
your sentiments. They flock to the polls and pass
the initiative into law.

What now?

Just picture the Brave New World that is created.
In fact, imagine the headlines if euthanasia *were*
legalized in this country:

> *Physicians are cast in the role of killer, not healer.*
> For 2400 years terminally ill, dying, and debilitated
> persons have had the assurance that doctors operate
> under an oath to heal them, not kill them. Under
> legalized euthanasia, the Hippocratic Oath is being

turned upside down and patient trust in doctors is seriously eroding. In fact, a fringe element in the medical community is beginning to act rashly, ending the lives of "difficult" patients rather than taking the time and effort to offer truly compassionate care.

Standard medical care is being seriously undermined. Elderly and severely disabled patients are not receiving the same quality of care as everyone else. Legalized euthanasia is resulting in less care for the dying, rather than better care as the medical community shifts its focus to cure and rehabilitation rather than care. It's a matter of economics: Euthanasia is extraordinarily cheap when compared with the costs of humane chronic and terminal care.

Legalized euthanasia establishes a fundamental right to die. The U.S. Constitution affirms that fundamental rights cannot be limited to any one group, such as the terminally ill. The door is now open to court challenges allowing suicide-on-demand for everyone: clinically depressed persons, children with cystic fibrosis, nursing home residents, people with AIDS, and those with large medical bills. Because all now enjoy an "equal protection of being killed," no one is denied aid in dying, especially those who cannot request it for themselves, such as people in comas or in persistent vegetative states.[4]

Legalized euthanasia broadens the application of the right to die. Vulnerable people, such as the poor, the senile, and those uninsured, are being pressured into euthanizing themselves in order to relieve the economic burden they place on society. Patients who are misdiagnosed are falling through the cracks of the new law. Many families are discovering that, without their knowledge, their loved ones are being killed.

The character of a helping society is beginning to disintegrate. Euthanasia is now seen as a cure-all to societal problems such as rising public health-care costs and limited facility space for elderly and debilitated people. It's easier to kill than cure, or even care. Society is now assigning no positive value to suffering and is becoming more oriented toward a culture of comfort. Discrimination against elderly and disabled people is beginning to run rampant—terms such as "useless victim" and "unfortunates to be pitied" reveal a growing cynicism and bigotry. Before euthanasia became legalized, hospice organizations and handicap associations had difficulty securing funding and volunteer support. Now, with the new law, these agencies are having more trouble than ever.

Legalized Euthanasia: A Good Law for a Better Society?

Does that Brave New World scenario sound farfetched?

Believe me, it's closer to home than you think. Right now in Europe there is a country where all this is beginning to happen. Although euthanasia is not legalized in Holland, the courts are turning a blind eye to thousands of terminally ill patients who are being euthanized by physicians. Some reports indicate that half the doctors in Holland who offer "aid in dying" have killed conscious patients without bothering to get consent.[5]

Perhaps you think that could never happen here in the good ol' U.S. of A.: "We would never let that occur in our country. Laws are meant to protect people, and legalizing euthanasia would just apply to those who want to die."

Not necessarily. The hotly emotional debate surrounding euthanasia underscores just how dynamic an issue it is. And dynamic issues in society never remain static, they are constantly evolving and laws are forever being revised to accommodate the changes. Advocates will say, "Well, right-to-die legislation was put on the books to *respond* to the terminally ill, but now we must *extend* the same legal rights to the comatose. And how about *amending* the law to include the severely mentally retarded? And AIDS is a pandemic so let's campaign to *modify* the law to include anyone who has the HIV virus."

I'm not being an alarmist. Even quadriplegics like me are at risk! "What can those of us who sympathize with a justified suicide by a handicapped person do to help?" asks Derek Humphry of The Hemlock Society. His answer gives me the jitters: "When we have statutes on the books permitting lawful physician aid-in-dying for the terminally ill, I believe that along with this reform there will come a more tolerant attitude toward other exceptional cases."[6]

No, I'm not a doomsday prophet when I say that

legalizing the right to die is like taking a crowbar to Pandora's box. Pry that lever under the lid with a single law and you've opened the whole box, exposing the entire population to "equal protection for being killed." Once legalized, the logical end of euthanasia is sheer terror. So why even get behind it in the first place?

There must be a better way. There has to be a different answer. No, I haven't forgotten the scenario that you're lying in bed with a terminal illness and facing perhaps a difficult and uncomfortable death in six months. And yes, I realize that we've yet to answer tough, distressing questions about tubes, machines, and life-support systems. But I won't abandon you after hospital visiting hours are over. I have more to say. I promise.

After all, "no man is an island entire of itself, every man is a piece of the Continent, a part of the main . . . any man's death diminishes me, because I am involved in mankind":

Dear Joni,

My name is Carol Walters. I was born with cerebral palsy—I walk with a limp and my hands I can use but I have poor control.

I was thinking how I don't think a handicapped person should take his or her life anymore than anyone else. I feel we are here to live our lives to contribute to our place where we live. Everyone has something to offer.

I have a part-time job at city hall in my town. At work I am known as Smiley. I clean up the community building and I sweep walks. I feel God has put me at that job for a reason. I think that reason is to help people realize that I can live a full and happy life the way I am.

I do have moments feeling sorry for myself and there are times I wish God would make me normal. I talk to my mom and she helps me see that I have many blessings.

Love,
Carol Walters

5

Your Decision Matters to You

We are now at the part where I wish there were no pages between us. I'd give anything if I could wheel up to your bedside past the bleeping machines and dripping tubes to talk face-to-face. Or be with you at your kitchen table to hear your heartache over your senile mother in a nursing home. Or just sit and listen as you lift the black cloak of depression long enough to speak.

If we were together, I'd want to talk about facing suffering: the kind that spins out of control, rips into your sanity, and tears apart your body—the kind of suffering that helpful information is powerless against.

If we were together, I'd want to peel back our defenses and confess how we both would really rather leapfrog the whole process of pain. How we'd like to detour the distress and shortcut the suffering. They say life is not something to be discarded when it does not work properly or seem to have value, but it is a constant struggle to hold onto it. How much easier to bypass it all.

Leapfrogging the Process of Pain

No thinking person chooses suffering. But we can choose our attitude in the midst of suffering.

That was a lesson driven home to me when years ago, in college, I read *Man's Search for Meaning*, a classic study of how people preserve their spiritual freedom and heroic responses in the face of horrible suffering. The author, Viktor Frankl, was a psychiatrist who was sent to a concentration camp in World War II where he found himself stripped to naked existence, cold, starved, beaten, and expecting extermination with each passing day. He lost his friends and family to the gas ovens. He lost every valued possession. How could he find life worth preserving?

The book hit home to me as a college student, even though campus life was far from the terrors of Auschwitz. But Viktor Frankl's work meant far more to me during the darkest, loneliest days of my two-year confinement in the hospital. There, lying face down strapped on a Stryker frame, I turned each page of *Man's Search for Meaning* with a mouthstick clutched between my teeth. My tears would drop and splatter on pages where this camp survivor wrote:

> We who lived in concentration camps can remember the men who walked through the huts comforting others, giving away their last piece of bread. They may have been few in number, but they offer sufficient proof that everything can be taken from a

man but one thing: the last of the human freedoms—to choose one's attitude in any given set of circumstances.

And there were always choices to make. Every day, every hour, offered the opportunity to make a decision, a decision to those powers which threatened to rob you of your very self, your inner freedom; which determined whether or not you would become the plaything of circumstance.

This man was worlds apart from my vocational rehab counselor. He had been there and so his words commanded my attention. I remember pausing to give my mouth a break from page turning, murmuring over and over, "I am *not* held hostage by my handicap. . . . I am *not* held hostage by my handicap." Mine was not so much a spiritual exercise but a mental effort, a first-step attempt at breaking free of the circumstances that dug their claws of control into me. I would read on:

> Even though conditions such as lack of sleep, insufficient food and various mental stresses may suggest that the inmates were bound to react in certain ways, in the final analysis it becomes clear that the sort of person the prisoner became was the result of an *inner decision*, and not the result of camp influences alone . . . When we are no longer able to change a situation—just think of an incurable disease such as inoperable cancer—we are challenged to change ourselves.[1]

I was challenged to change myself. But how? I felt a little sheepish that my inner decision could barely move me to smile in my wheelchair, let alone face with courage things like starvation, beatings, and gas ovens.

When I finished Viktor Frankl's book, I realized it was an answer to one basic question, a question that in fact the psychiatrist, after he was released and returned to his practice, often asked his troubled patients: "Why do you not commit suicide?"

In other words, "Why do you not leapfrog suffering?"

From their answers it was then the goal of the psychiatrist to weave these slender threads of a broken life into a pattern of meaning. Each person, he insisted, could find valuable meaning in suffering.

I mused over the meaning to my suffering while lying right side up on my Stryker frame rather than upside down—it was easier to think hopeful thoughts facing fresh air than the floor! As I counted the tiles on the ceiling, I counted the few, slender, bright-shining threads of my broken life.

I'm alive.

I can at least still feel in my neck and tops of my shoulders.

I can see the moon through my hospital window.

I'm learning that patience and endurance means more on a Stryker frame than running twenty-five laps around a hockey field.

My friends are still coming to see me, and the doughnuts they bring taste good. It's nice to have the nurse read me Robert Frost's poetry during her lunch break. I like listening to the Beatles.

And, like holding on to a thin kite string, I have hope that it might get better. I see it in the eyes and smiles of my family, my friends, and a few of the nurses. Oh, and one more positive thing—they might find a cure for spinal cord injury!

Small as they were, these slender threads tied me to life, even if I hadn't yet decided if it was worth living. The threads were fragile, but they held me through the day and kept me connected to people. The meaning behind it all, however, was still unclear. But I knew this much: It had something to do with God.

Someone said if you believe that the individual is supreme, then your responsibility is only to yourself since there is no God who gives us life or who awaits us in death. But if you believe that life derives from a loving Creator, then leapfrogging the suffering process must be considered within a larger context.[2]

It was a fact that my background oriented me toward God. And my assessment about life and death was becoming a matter of conscience rather than a knee-jerk reaction to the problems at hand. Weeks passed. My thoughts deepened. And the longer I hung in there through the process of suffering, the stronger the weave in the fabric of meaning. I was convinced God was mysteriously behind the pattern, so I took a closer look at new threads.

My friendships are deepening and becoming more honest.

What's important in life is people.

I'm learning the value of a smile.

God is real. I can feel Him when I'm alone at night.

There are others who are hurting a lot more than me and I'm beginning to care, honestly care, about them.

What were once thin, slender threads were now becoming cords. And the fabric of meaning behind my suffering was beginning to take shape. Life, I was discovering, was worth living.

Talking About the "G" Word

I know I've brought up a delicate subject for some. Even medical ethicists all but banish God from their discussions and writings. And those who help set moral and medical standards in hospitals tend to confine the subject of God to the hospital chapel. But let's be honest—prayer and God are as commonplace in hospitals as bedpans and bottles of pills.

So let's have a quick rehab lesson here. Traditional rehabilitation philosophy will pull out all the stops to address a patient's physical, psychological, emotional, and vocational needs, while spiritual needs are at best ignored. But more professionals are beginning to see that the rehabilitation of a person's spirit is key in affecting all those other areas. A healthy and whole spirit affects everything from a patient's attitude and motivation to his everyday relationships. Why? Because how a person relates to God has a profound influence on what he thinks about himself, his goals, and his friends and family. It has something to do with responding to "higher authority" and a source of "absolute value."

A disabled person who connects with God usually demonstrates personal freedom, responsibility to the community, true achievement, and meaningful relationships with people. And what if a person ignores God and sets himself up at the center of his own moral universe? Well, those who remain masters of their own lives to the exclusion of God and others will inevitably negate themselves. As the Vatican papers have stated, "Man, who is alienated from the Source of Life, his Creator, expresses his dominion over his own life by destroying it."

Of course, theologians would jump in here and have much more to say, but for now it's safe to underscore that relating with God can bring about the foundational stability of peace in a patient's life. Peace with the One in charge ... peace with circumstances ... and peace with one's self.

Is Weaving the Threads Worth the Effort?

So much for me. And so much for Viktor Frankl.

But a death camp survivor and a quadriplegic simply can't paste our experiences on others who want to leapfrog their suffering. What would Viktor Frankl say to someone like Larry McAfee, a civil engineer paralyzed from the neck down by a 1985 motorcycle accident and sustained on a ventilator?

And what could I say to Larry McAfee? Unable to move out of a nursing home, and unable to breathe on his own, Larry asked the courts to allow him to pull the plug on his ventilator and die. The court petition simply stated that Larry "has no control over his person and receives no enjoyment out of life."[3]

I wasted no time in writing Larry.

Dear Larry,

> Like you, I've experienced being reduced to just existing—the basics of breathing, eating and sleeping. Lying there, I felt as though my experience represented every human (it's just that the rest of the human race didn't realize they were merely breathing and sleeping—they were too busy being on their feet with a lot of distractions). After much thinking I realized that there *had* to be more to life for everybody than just mere existence. And if not, then why not everybody "pull the plug" no matter if they were disabled or not!

In a way, I felt as though Viktor Frankl were looking over my shoulder from his bunkbed in that concentration camp. He too would agree that there had to be more to life than just existing, going through the motions, getting born and then growing old and then dying. But I wanted to take it a step further from the advice of the psychiatrist; I wanted to talk to Larry about how I connected with God.[4]

At that point, I came to the conclusion that there had to be a personal God who cared for me and everybody else if, indeed, life was to make sense. There must be a God . . . and if not, then the whole human race should put a gun to its head if it wants to. But humans are too unique, too significant to just put ourselves out of our misery if we can't handle suffering. No, there must be a God who cares. There must be.

As I wrote, I wished there were no pages between Larry and me. I would have given anything to wheel into his room and angle my chair close to his bed so he could see me through the tubes and machines. If we were together, I'd confess how I, too, at one time wanted to leapfrog the process of pain.

And I would tell Larry that God knew exactly how we both felt. God wasn't holed up in an ivory tower in the corner of the universe. He suffered, too. Even Jesus was tempted to give in. He even sought, if possible, to avoid the suffering of the cross, pleading, " 'Father, if You are willing, take this cup from me.' " In the Garden of Gethsemane as the shadow of His death approached, He felt alone and distressed with no one around who could understand. So He turned to His Father, the only one He could talk to, "And being in anguish, he prayed more earnestly."[5]

I would also tell Larry that Jesus' decision to face the cross squarely secured a deeper meaning for the suffering of us all. More meaning than we could possibly imagine.

As I dropped my letter to Larry into the mailbox, I hoped he would find his own few bright-shining threads of meaning. But virtually the next day I saw a headline in the newspaper, "Judge rules quadriplegic can end life at will." My shoulders slumped when I also read, "The ventilator to which he is attached is not prolonging his life; it is prolonging his death," said the judge. A petition included an affidavit stating "I understand turning off the ventilator will result in my death," signed by a shaky "X" made with a pencil held in McAfee's mouth.[6]

That made me, an activist and advocate, steaming mad! If that judge had been approached by a poor minority woman who could no longer endure racism, sexism, and poverty, and she wanted aid to end her life painlessly, the woman would have been refused flat-out. In fact, she would be offered support in seeking better housing and a job. But when a disabled person like Larry McAfee declares the same intention, people assume he is acting rationally.

Back to Larry's story. What happened next was a little confusing. For some reason he decided not to have himself removed from the respirator. Next, Larry was transferred from the nursing home to another facility. His story dropped out of the papers and I was unable to hunt up his new address. I had no idea where Larry was or what he was thinking, but I kept pulling for him from a distance, hoping that he would find those threads of meaning for his life.

Finally, after several years, I tracked him down. I was itching to find out why he decided to live, so I called him up. We chatted for a few moments, talking about quadriplegia and pressure sores, and then I got a little more serious. "Larry," I asked, "why did you decide not to follow through on assisted suicide? What was your reason to keep on living?"

He managed to speak in between huffs and puffs of his respirator. "Because I'm not forced to live in an institution or hospital anymore. I'm living in a little independent living house with two other guys in wheelchairs. It's a lot more enjoyable with a lot less pressure, less rigid. You can set your own schedule. As long as I'm not forced to live under the conditions of the state, then I consider life worth living."

My eyes lit up. I inhaled deeply and then let it out slowly. He was right. Too many debilitated people feel trapped, even warehoused in institutions. Saving people's lives and rehabilitating them is pointless if they are denied the means to control their lives. I prodded him a bit more. "So it's a chance to forge friendships, pursue hobbies?"

"Yeah, just to feel more human."

"What was it like in the institution?"

Larry paused a moment. "I just existed from day to day. But here I'm able to meet people on an equal basis."

This man sounded like he found his bright-shining threads. Slender, just a few, but threads strong

enough to weave meaning into his life. As I listened,
I kept whispering thanks under my breath. As John
Donne had written, Larry's death would have di-
minished me, especially me, another quadriplegic!

I dared one more question. "Any advice you can
give to people who, like you and me, can't use their
hands or legs, maybe in wheelchairs?"

The line was quiet and I could tell he was
thinking. "I'll be honest. If a person, after years of
trying, feels like he can't go on, then I feel it's
within his right to . . . well, you know."

My spirits sagged a little. But I was thankful that
he, at least, felt like he *could* go on. And I took
comfort from the fact that his decision to live had
most assuredly inspired others to do the same. Just
then Larry added, "But I'd tell them, 'Don't rush
into any hasty decisions but give things a lot of
thought and time. Don't try to conform to society.
Give it time. Seek some guidance, not only from
God but friends and family.'"

Friends.

Family.

God.

These were the bright-shining threads in his life.
Warm, caring, available people who accepted him,
brought him out of social isolation, listened to his
anger, helped him discover truth about himself, and
encouraged him to interpret his future as a friend.[7]

How did they do it? They were people who
circumvented the crippling health-care system that
had sentenced him to an institution and denied him

the self-determination to live independently. They were the people who put together the concept of the little independent-living center, who recognized Larry's freedom to set his own schedule and live as he wished. They were people who became his friends at the center, and from what he said at the close of our phone conversation, perhaps even helped him find God.[8]

Larry learned what every hurting person who chooses life discovers: *Answers most often come in the form of people rather than sentences.*

Helpful Information and . . .

People. I don't think Larry would have made it without them. His was a burden that needed bearing. His misery needed mercy. He didn't need an argument, a rational discussion, or placement in a suicide-prevention program. What he needed was a few people ready to give practical love, the kind of love that has its sleeves rolled up. And Larry's friends weren't the type to point him to a cross-stitched proverb set behind glass in a pretty frame. They helped him live information, love it, fight it, breathe it, and make it his own.

Men and women said to Larry, "Choose life."
Friends said to me, "Believe in God."
Even Viktor Frankl said to thousands in despair, "Suffering can have meaning."
And thankfully, these people did not wad up truths into platitudes to be tossed at us who hurt,

while they stood at a respectable arm's-length distance. "Believe in God" glowed with the warm heartbeat of love that was as real as flesh and blood. "Choose life" were words spoken straight ahead with a smile that involved, that invited. "Suffering can have meaning" was the covering that gently enfolded.

Helpful information is not enough. No one comes out of despair alive without a caring friend on the other side. For . . .

> Two are better than one, because they have a good return for their work: If one falls down, his friend can help him up. But pity the man who falls and has no one to help him up!
>
> Ecclesiastes 4:9–10

You cannot, you must not suffer alone. It matters to the point of life and death.

6

Your Decision Matters to the Enemy

I'll never forget the first day of my marriage to Ken. What a carefree, delightful morning!

As our jet lifted off from Los Angeles to fly us to our honeymoon in Hawaii, we cuddled and kissed. The flight attendants giggled and presented us with a cake and a couple of leis. After they served refreshments, we settled back and put on the earphones to watch the in-flight movie. To my surprise it was *Whose Life Is It Anyway?*, the film about a quadriplegic who tried to get everyone from his friends to his doctor to his lawyer to permit him the right to die.

Ken and I pulled off our earphones. This was not the time to think about the depression of quadriplegia or the desire it often brings to cut one's life short.

As the opening credits appeared on the screen, the flight attendant knelt by my seat and whispered, "Oh, Mrs. Tada, I'm very sorry about the movie selection today. Shall we change your seat?"

I smiled and shook my head no. I knew I had hope and a future, although I had a difficult time the rest of the flight convincing the attendants that I was not bothered by the visual images on the screen. Yet even as Ken and I snuggled and talked of our future, I kept sneaking peeks at the film.

Without the soundtrack, strange and twisted thoughts began to whisper and wheedle into my brain. *Does Ken really know what he's gotten himself into? What if we can't handle it? Divorce and suicide happen to couples like us all the time. What if . . .*

Hold it! This was the happiest day of my life, and I refused to entertain such deplorable thoughts! I shook my head, jerked my attention away from the movie, and riveted it totally on Ken. I wasn't about to allow subtle ideas, like flying birds, to build a nest in my head.

It's called resisting temptation.

A provoking thought. A strong inclination. An inducement, an enticement to give in and give up. A crazy idea that settles in and begins to sound pleasing and plausible.

Thoughts leading to death begin that way.

I've had enough experience with temptation to know that such provocations aren't furtive ideas that dart out of nowhere, disjointed and having no connection. There exists an intelligence behind those ideas. Such thoughts are part of a deadly scheme, the end of which is always death.

I can just hear some say, "She believes there exists an 'intelligence' behind evil? What is she, illiterate? This sounds like something out of *The Twilight Zone.*"

In case you think I sound uncool, stop and consider. One glance at the track record of moral evil in this world's hall of history horrors should convince you that it smells of something systematized. And systems don't just happen. They are devised. They are schemed. Behind them is intelligence.

Judaism, Christianity, Buddhism, Islam—they all recognize an intelligence behind moral evil.

Little wonder Jesus not only believed in a devil, but nailed him with the name "tempter." Jesus called him that when the devil enticed Him to stand on the highest point of the temple and throw Himself down.[1]

And the tempter had one goal: murder. That's why, later on, Jesus nailed him again: "He was a murderer from the beginning, not holding to the truth, for there is no truth in him. When he lies, he speaks his native language, for he is a liar and the father of lies."[2]

The Tempter. Murderer from the beginning. Father of lies. The devil's goal is to destroy your life, either by making your existence a living nightmare, or by pushing you into an early grave. Take heed: If you have ever been enticed to prematurely end your life, then you've been listening not just to something but to someone. And just what are a few of the tempting lies he whispers?

"No One Cares"

One afternoon a couple of weeks ago, I was sitting at my friend's coffee table, wrestling with whether or not I should tell her about the depression that had gripped me for several days. I decided to open up.

"Do you have time to listen?" I asked.

"Sure," she said, and promptly rose to retrieve a whistling teakettle from the stove. As she poured, I took a deep breath and started to unfold my problem.

Pause. "Milk in your tea?" Nod yes. Start again. Phone rings. "Wait a minute." Pick up where we left off. Knock at door. "What were you saying?" More distractions.

Friend half-listens. Friend gets up to warm tea. Help. I hurt. And this person could care less.

C. Samuel Storms said,

> Beneath the water-line of every life are the frustrated longings, sinful schemes, thoughts and fantasies of a fallen soul . . . here are where people are hurting. Tragically, we rarely encounter one another at that level. . . . How adept we have become in our ability to get along without one another.[3]

It's true. Some people could care less. Friends get preoccupied . . . nurses rush by your bed to the next patient . . . neighbors never venture across the street to see how you're doing . . . families move apart and connect only occasionally over the phone.

In fact, you may feel no one cares for you. If so,

those feelings might be justified. I've wheeled down nursing home hallways, peered into rooms, and have grieved to see lonely people sitting and staring, waiting for someone to visit them. Or you may be a lonely person who rubs shoulders with plenty of people all the time but have no intimate contact with them. Discussion about weather and sports may fill your day while the real issues, the kind that eat at you when you lie awake thinking at night, stay harbored inside. You think, *Does anyone care?*

There *are* people who care. And it's possible you have built a self-imposed wall around you, a wall that allows absolutely no one inside to see what you're going through and to hurt with your hurts.

Your Creator never intended that you should shoulder a load of suffering by yourself. That's the whole purpose of spiritual community—God deliberately designed people to need each other. We must rub shoulders with people of hope and faith if our innermost needs are to be met.

And what if your relationships with those few friends aren't as open or as dependable as you'd like them to be? Then it may be up to you to do something about it. A community of people who give the kind of love that "has its sleeves rolled up" can be created, if not found! A spontaneous, warm connection could develop with the chaplain in the hospital . . . a new friendship could happen with the kindly woman who visits your roommate . . . a fellowship could grow with those one or two people you always see praying in the hospital chapel . . . or maybe caring people could be found in that support group you've been avoiding.

That caring person may be a relative who is not so distant. An old friend you almost forgot about. A co-worker who used to invite you to lunch now and then. People who care can be found in homeless shelters. Churches. Meetings of Alcoholics Anonymous. Parents Without Partners. Weight Watchers. Handicap associations.

Someone cares. That fact was driven home when Terry Anderson, the American journalist held hostage for over six years, was released out of Lebanon. Isolated in a cell, blindfolded and abused, he had every reason to think no one cared. But the few snippets of BBC broadcasts over which he heard his sister's voice were all he needed. Someone cared. And although he could only imagine his sister's embrace, he knew a friend was on the other side of his despair. That thought alone helped him get through.

"There's Nothing More to Expect from Life"

This is another standard lie and it's a tempting thought, especially when you can't see beyond the thick, gray fog of hopelessness that has settled around you. But it's still a lie. There is life on the other side of that fog.

Viktor Frankl put it this way:

> In the concentration camp, I remember two cases of would-be suicide which bore a striking similarity.

Both used the typical argument—they had nothing more to expect from life. In both cases it was a question of getting them to realize that *life was still expecting something from them.* . . .

For one, it was his child whom he adored . . . for the other it was a thing, not a person. This man was a scientist and had written a series of books which still needed to be finished. A man who becomes conscious of the responsibility he bears toward a human being who affectionately waits for him, or to an unfinished work, will never be able to throw away his life. He knows the "why" for his existence, and will be able to bear almost any "how."[4]

You may not be expecting anything from life, but life is still anticipating something from you. Like the man in the concentration camp, your responsibility may be to a child, perhaps a grandchild or the young boy down the street. Your decision to die or not to die has a powerful impact on the mind of a boy or girl.

In the movie *The Boy Who Could Fly*, the father who felt he had nothing to give ended his life prematurely, leaving two children. His son became withdrawn and sullen. Leaning on his elbows, the teary-eyed boy mumbled about his father's demise, "He didn't even try to fight . . . he just gave up . . . he didn't try." The father's decision had a lasting and negative impact on that child's life.

In a different example a friend of mine named Carol Swegle had everything: a rich husband, a beauty queen title, a gorgeous country home, wealthy friends, and loving children. But Carol became depressed and tried to find relief in a combination of prescription drugs and alcohol. She had pinned all her hopes on a little bit of fame and a small fortune only to discover emptiness. One day in her bedroom, she placed a gun in her mouth and readied herself to pull the trigger. At that instant her children burst into the room and startled her. The gun went off.

Carol fell to the floor, a quadriplegic. She lost her husband, her house, her friends and ended up living in a nursing home. If ever there was a time to pull a trigger, it would have been then! But Carol hung on to the hope of claiming back her children. Her daughters gave her reason enough to try again. In the end? Although it was true her children had been adversely affected by her suicide attempt, in the long run, through Carol's perseverance and changed attitude, her decision to live became her children's redemption. They were reunited.

Life, perhaps in a child, is still expecting something from you.

Then again, life, perhaps in a thing, is anticipating more from you. I receive letters from prisoners, disabled people in institutions, and elderly folks who often send poems, small paintings, crayoned drawings, crocheted bookmarkers, pot holders . . . whatever. These things are expressions of an individual to me, another person. Scribbled drawings and tattered bookmarks are expressions of the soul, and these simple things tie this person to the rest of the world.

"I Can't Live With This Depression"

You don't have to believe that lie. Admittedly nothing distorts reality like depression. A blowup with your husband has you discounting twenty years of a good marriage. A little headache has you wondering if you've got brain cancer. A diagnosis of a serious illness has you digging your grave the next day. It's amazing how quickly reality gets turned upside down when you're depressed.

But I was impressed with the way this teenager approached her depression:

Dear Joni,

My name is Katherine and I'll be fourteen in four days. It also marks my first year in my wheelchair. I've lost the use of my legs and one arm forever. (The arm part is my own fault though.) I wouldn't do my therapy because I was so depressed over my bleak future.

Now I've discovered I need God's love more than ever. I want to start off talking with someone who knows what I'm going through. Please help me find the love a Christian knows.

Katherine is barely in her teens, has lived in a wheelchair for virtually a year, and yet devotes not more than one line to her depression. Most of us would devote an entire page!

When I wrote Katherine back, I shared how even stained-glass window saints like the apostles got depressed. The apostle Paul wrote to his friends in a letter,

> We are pressed on every side by troubles, but not crushed and broken. We are perplexed because we don't know why things happen as they do, but we don't give up and quit. We get knocked down, but we get up again and keep going.[5]

There's a little bit of that attitude in Katherine. Somehow after hitting rock bottom, she was able to get up again and keep going. I'm sure it took time to work through her sorrow, grief, and limitations, but somewhere in the fog of hopelessness, she found a thin ray of hope.

It's called faith. You don't need much more than the mustard-seed-sized faith of a fourteen-year-old girl. True, Katherine, like most of us, will face even tougher times in the future, but she has begun to learn to choose her attitude and to invest her life in others. In so doing, she will be able to live no matter what her feelings.

"Nothing Awaits Me After Death"

This could be the biggest lie of all.

And this is exactly why the devil enjoys helping you scheme your own murder. Does that sound harsh? You may call it self-deliverance or euthanasia if you wish; it matters little to the devil. It's all murder to him.

Also it matters little whether or not you believe in hell. Again the devil doesn't care whether you label it "a white light at the end of a tunnel," or "nirvana," or "never-never land." It's all hell to him.

And what is it like? Fire and brimstone? A black hole? A bleak nothingness? Again the devil shrugs his shoulders at such descriptions. All that matters to him is that hell is separation, total and final, from God. Hell is misery, more deep and profound than any misery you could experience on earth. And because misery loves company, the devil wants to take as many with him to hell as he possibly can. That includes you.

Frankly it's enough that Jesus believed in hell, and he spoke of it more often than He did of heaven. Without going into a lot of detail here, Jesus simply warned, "It is better for you to enter life maimed or crippled than to have two hands or two feet and be thrown into eternal fire."[6]

The tempter would have you believe that it's not that bad a place. And just how does the devil beguile you into hell before you can find heaven? His strategy reminds me of a letter I read recently that described advice given to a man dying from AIDS:

Dear Editor,

A terminally ill AIDS patient recently called the Hemlock Society of North Texas. He was suffering greatly . . . in our phone conversations his anguish over the conviction that he would probably go to hell also came out.

I told him of my own and other beliefs, which differ greatly, on this subject. I described a recent survey which shows that about fifty percent of all Americans believe in the existence of hell, but only about four percent think they are likely to go there. With the help from my friendly local librarian, I obtained a copy of this survey to send him, along with the Drug Dosage Table of the National Hemlock Society.

This may be the first time the Society has helped someone to carry out a "double self-deliverance," both from a harsh terminal illness and from a harsh theological conviction.

The Hemlock Society of North Texas[7]

This person with AIDS was told the truth about how to kill himself with lethal drugs, but he wasn't told the truth about hell. The letter was an eerie cover-up of the facts. Do you believe that nothing awaits you after death? Would you be willing to stake your life on it? Of all the questions to be settled before you take the final exit, this issue is paramount.

If you think that hell is fiction, then say so. Don't be like the fifty percent of Americans who believe in hell, but claim it's not their destiny. If you have even an inkling that it may be real, then wake up. Leave no stone unturned, no means untried until you find life worth living both on this side of eternity and on the other.

Don't Believe Lies

The devil will go to any lengths to charm you into an early grave. Everything from pushing drug dosage tables in your face, to pooh-poohing hell as pure nonsense. He'll move all of hell (and heaven if he could) to stop your heartbeat and have you pronounced dead.

Let's unmask his way of operating.

This morning I was having a rough start getting out of bed. My paralysis was giving me fits. I shook my head and growled, "This body is a pain. I hate it!"

Why was that so awful? Because the enemy has a deep hatred of my body and all I was doing was agreeing with him. He gets a charge out of my verbal barbs about my body. And he would like to get you to do the same. Whether you are approaching the final throes of a terminal illness, or whether you're deep in depression, the devil delights in hearing us bad-mouth our bodies.

Why? Because your body, even underneath wrinkles or fat, and in spite of the ravages of illness or old age, is made in the image of God. Your heart, mind, hands, and feet are stamped with the imprint of the Creator. Little wonder the devil wants you to do your body in!

This morning I had to, once again, plug my ears against the lies of the tempter and remember that I am "fearfully and wonderfully made."[8] I rehearsed the old, familiar truth that God has a plan for this flesh and blood of mine. That's why the devil considers my body a threat. He understands that when I yield to God my body, albeit paralyzed, my feet and hands are powerful weapons against his forces of darkness.

Listen to the Truth

By the way, the devil would have you believe a couple more lies. He wants to convince you that he is either a powerless elf-gone-bad in a red suit with a funny tail, or an evenly matched and almost-as-mighty opponent of God.

Neither is true.

The devil is only a fallen angel.[9]

He is a deceiver.[10]

He is doomed for destruction.[11]

And until then, he has one goal in mind: your destruction.

7

Your Decision Matters to God

Some people would look at Diane Sabol sitting in her big, bulky wheelchair, stiff and motionless, and shake their heads. She has to be fed everything and pushed everywhere. The creeping limitations of her multiple sclerosis have curled her fingers, making them stiff and rigid. Her voice is barely a whisper. Often she has to stay in bed.

"Why doesn't she just end it all?" some people say. Diane struggled through the diagnosis of her disease, an ensuing divorce, and a custody battle for her children. Then she went through more paralysis and pain only to be forced by her MS to lose her children again. From there she went downhill to a lonely and dreary existence in an institution. "I didn't want to live to see my fortieth birthday," Diane recalls.

Things are much better now for Diane. Somewhere in the midst of hopelessness, Diane was able to connect with one or two nurse's aides. A fragile friendship slowly strengthened with one aide named Connie and, several years later, Diane was able to move into a small apartment with the help of her new friend. Diane saw Connie as an answer to prayer. In fact, she began to see that her life was worth living because of two things: people and God. "Now on this my fiftieth year of life, I'm looking forward to the years ahead," she told me recently.

Diane still spends all of her time either in her wheelchair or bed. Her paralysis is getting worse. Her vision is dimming. Yet Diane finds satisfaction in her work. In fact, others literally depend on her for finding life worth living. She spends hours at work, reaching out to the gangs in the streets of east L.A.: aiding homeless mothers, single parents, abused children, despondent teenagers, and the dying and forgotten old people in the nursing home where she once lived. She works to move mountains that block the paths of Peace Corps workers in Latin America and help open the eyes of the spiritually blind in Southeast Asia.

No, Diane doesn't run a crisis hotline. Her telephone wires are invisible but no less real; and her work, although spiritual, is accomplishing just as much as if she were talking one-on-one with homeless mothers, gang members, and abused children. Diane's work is to pray.

This meek and quiet woman sees her place in the world; it doesn't matter that others may not recognize her significance in the grand scheme of things. Her motto? "The point of this life . . . is to become the person God can love perfectly, to satisfy His thirst to love. Being counts more than doing, the singer more than the song. We had better stop looking for escape hatches, for this is our hatchery."[1]

"Finally," Diane says, "I've found peace."

Perhaps you're not slumped in a big bulky wheelchair. You may not even be dying, debilitated, or terminally ill. But still you'd give anything to feel the peace Diane has found. Trouble is, you might be tempted to still believe the lie that peace is found by prematurely ending your life.

True, you may feel that no one seems to care. And maybe not a soul does care! You may feel as though life is not expecting a single thing from you, and you simply cannot live with depression. Sadly you are even willing to stake your life on the belief that nothing awaits you after death.

If so, you *need* peace! But remember, peace of mind comes not in the form of sentences but people. There is a Person who cares about you, even if no one else does. He calls Himself the Prince of Peace. And it is His perspective on life I want to talk to you about.

The Bible Speaks Out on Euthanasia

You may think that euthanasia of dying or debilitated people is a rather recent phenomenon, but not so. The Old Testament records an incident involving King Saul of Israel, who became seriously wounded on the battlefield. Fearing the advancing enemy, Saul took his own sword and tried to fall against it. He cried to a soldier, "Come and put me out of my misery for I am in terrible pain but life lingers on."

The soldier deferred to the wishes of the king and killed him. Then acting most likely on his innocence, he brought some of Saul's armor to David and said, "I killed him, for I knew he couldn't live."[2]

There were no laws on the books back then about assisted suicide, but that did not stop David from banging the gavel of Israel's justice. He ordered the soldier put to death. Perhaps onlookers were shocked by the verdict. After all, Saul was dying anyway, he was in great pain, and if captured, he feared torture and abuse in his final hours. These things were probably on the mind of the soldier who performed the mercy killing, but his actions stand in contrast with Saul's bodyguard who, minutes earlier, was too terrified to commit the act.[3]

To be fair, it seems that Saul's status as king of Israel added to the guilt of the deed, and David was outraged that someone had the nerve to harm the king who was anointed of God. But I believe it's fair to draw a principle that is as true for people today as for people living several thousand years ago. Whether a monarch or a common man, mercy killing anybody is wrong; Saul's being king only heightened the criminality of the soldier's deed.[4]

God clearly opposes *active euthanasia*, whether it be plunging a sword into the bleeding body of a king on a battlefield, or plunging a syringe full of phenobarbital into the veins of a dying patient. The prohibition against murder in the Ten Commandments logically includes murder of the self. Mercy killing and suicide contradict the legitimate self-love of "love your neighbor as *yourself*."[5]

As far as *passive euthanasia* is concerned, there's no biblical account of someone withdrawing medical treatment to cause death, an act that constitutes passive euthanasia. But it's not hard to imagine that had King Saul been rescued by paramedics and put on life supports, only to have some Amalekite unplug them, God would have frowned. Mercy killing, whether committed actively or passively, is always presented in a negative light in the Bible. In Scripture, people who either killed themselves or sought to be put out of their misery are always seen as disobedient.[6]

And as far as those who will say, "I'll do with my body as I wish," God has a response: "You are not your own, therefore honor God with your body."[7]

In short, any means to produce death in order to alleviate suffering is never justified. Or in the language of the Bible, it is never right to do evil.[8]

The Bible Speaks Out on Dying

However, *letting someone die* is another matter entirely. Allowing a person to die when he is, in fact, dying is justified. The Bible is full of examples of people doing all they can to help a person live, but when it came time to die, Scripture doesn't do much more than record the death. No paramedics called to the scene, no CPR, no Heimlich maneuver.

The Old and New Testaments do not specifically address many of our present-day problems and questions related to "letting someone die." Scripture is probably silent because those problems didn't exist in biblical times. The absence of respirators, drug therapies, heart pumps, and feeding tubes did not confuse the difference between prolonging the process of dying and sustaining life.

In fact, the Bible speaks about death not in technical terms, but in the everyday language of ordinary experience. Today, doctors would agree a person is dead if the functions of the brain and brain stem cease, but Scripture does not formally define death in those terms or any others. It simply assumes we understand what death is.

But what Scripture lacks in absolute definitions, it makes up for in absolute decrees. There's a kind of medical dictionary exactness to a verse like Job 14:5, "Man's days are determined; you have decreed the number of his months and have set limits he cannot exceed."

That verse, and others, rightly influence our judgments. "Keeping a comatose person who has an incurable disease alive on a machine when he is irreversibly dying is unnecessary," says evangelical theologian Norman L. Geisler in his book *Christian Ethics*. "In fact, it could be viewed as unethical. . . . Extraordinary efforts to fight the divinely appointed limits of our mortality are really working in opposition to God."[9]

Trade Fear In for Peace

People's intense interest in euthanasia can be summed up in one word: fear. Ever since the days of Eden, we've been haunted by fear of each side of the grave we look at. Like the old song goes, "I'm tired of living, but scared of dying." On this side of the tombstone, our fears are aggravated by strange new diseases, machines that dehumanize, and treatments that rob dignity. Yet peering beyond the tombstone, we're afraid of that scary left turn into hell.

Peace is the opposite of fear. As I shared, we are all in search of peace when it comes to life-and-death decisions. And the Prince of Peace is the only one who can rid you of fear no matter which side of the grave you look at. The Bible calms our fears when it says:

> Since we, God's children, are human beings—made of flesh and blood—he became flesh and blood too by being born in human form; for only as a human being could he die and in dying break the power of the devil who had the power of death. Only in that way could he deliver those who through fear of death have been living all their lives as slaves to constant dread.[10]

Read it again. God became a human being—that's Jesus. Jesus, through His death, broke the power of the devil and his lies. He also wants to deliver you of your fears, whether fear of life as a living nightmare or fear of death as a permanent and total separation from God. To believe in Jesus gives you peace in the here and now and peace about the hereafter.

How? Well, remember that scary left turn into hell? What makes it so foreboding is our guilt. And guilt is no psychological fiction: You've broken Somebody's law and no matter how much others may flatter you on the outside, on the inside a guilty conscience nails you for lust, pride, and prejudice, just to name a few. The punishment for breaking the law is death. But like the verse says, Jesus *delivers!* When He bore God's punishment, Jesus raised His cross as a sign marker, arranging a right turn away from hell and into heaven.

To place your hand in the Prince of Peace's hand does not necessarily guarantee you protection from suffering, nor does it offer immunity from difficult deathbed decisions. But it does give you a steadfast hand to hold onto, including the certainty that a loving and all-powerful God who knows everything is standing by your side. Putting your confidence in Christ will free you from living all your life as a slave to constant dread. Dread of facing life as a living nightmare, and dread of facing death as the dark unknown.

God loves life; God despises death for "the last enemy to be destroyed is death."[11] Jesus said, "My purpose is to give life in all its fullness"—life not only in the here and now, but in the hereafter.[12] There are good reasons why God wants you to live: He wants you to have peace, He knows your life can have value in the here and now, and He wants you to make that right turn into heaven.

God Knows You're Heading for a Hereafter

If you were to ask Diane Sabol which truth from the Bible gave her the most peace, she might say, "I consider that our present sufferings are not worth comparing with the glory that will be revealed in us."[13]

That's saying a mouthful! Some people find it difficult to think realistically about heaven. Even the spiritually minded feel awkward working toward "eternity" because it seems so far away, almost unreal. Even when we try to imagine what it would be like, we come up short of a real desire to go there. Who wants to live forever tucked behind a galaxy where birds chirp, organs play, and angels bounce from cloud to cloud?

If that were a true picture of heaven, an awful lot of people besides Diane would be lukewarm about going there.

The fact is, descriptions about heaven aren't as important as grasping the *fact* of heaven. Heaven is the place where God is going to give His family the biggest welcome-home party in history. Entrance into heaven means no more suffering, no more tears, and a life free from pain and filled with joy. Perhaps that's why people who are dying, debilitated, or terminally ill are often those most ready to believe in God. Maybe the devil could care less about whether or not you believe in hell, but God definitely cares whether or not you believe in heaven! Your eternal destiny rests on it.

Believing in Jesus is the first step to a life that goes far beyond this world. Once that is settled, there are a few facts we can hold onto until we cross the other side of the grave and step into a brighter eternity with God.

You were made for one purpose, and that is to make God real to those around you. Don't think He has left you without any means whatever for fulfilling that end, just because you are confined to bed or struggling with pain. In a mysterious way each day that you live, each hopeful thought you think, however fleeting, each smile you muster brings God incredible joy. That's because your positive attitude and actions, however small and faint, are fingers pointing others to a God who is larger and finer and grander than they thought. That's what it means to glorify Him as you lie in that bed, sit in that wheelchair, or persevere through that depression.

Your suffering has meaning now and forever. This is what Diane's favorite verse is all about. Your present suffering isn't worth comparing with the glory that will be revealed in you. How can that be? Loneliness, feelings of total abandonment, pain, and the like are capable of being exchanged for something precious, eternal, weighty, and real—so much so that it's hardly worth comparing the two. God will one day reward you for sticking through suffering with an uncomplaining attitude. When you exchange the anger for faith in Him, then your life in heaven will be larger, finer, and grander because of that very suffering.

God works in your life up until the final moment. It may appear that nothing is taking place in the life of a dying loved one, a comatose individual, or a severely incapacitated person, but God is not hindered from accomplishing His work in a life just because it seems nothing is happening. The work of God is spiritual activity, often far separate from one's brain, neurological, or muscular activity. Only eternity will reveal the work that was accomplished.

Life is more fleeting than we realize. We act as though this world is all there is. It's little wonder we don't care about eternity. We need the perspective of the psalmist who said:

Show me, O Lord, my life's end and the number of my days; let me know how fleeting is my life. You have made my days a mere handbreadth; the span of my years is as nothing before you . . . Man is a mere phantom as he goes to and fro: He bustles about, but only in vain; he heaps up wealth, not knowing who will get it.[14]

The shortness of life ought to open our eyes to what it means to live beyond time. When you put your pain in that perspective, time not only seems shortened, but suffering has an end in sight.

Dying is your final passage. The stripping of all human powers, mental as well as physical, is a part of the process that George MacDonald calls "undressing for the last sweet bed." When we who believe in God die, we leave behind our permanent claim on our earthly "clothes" and we are "clothed upon" with immortality.[15]

God knows you're heading for a hereafter. For those who, apart from Him, prematurely end their lives hoping to find relief there will only be a hereafter of vast and utter disappointment. For those who believe in Jesus, the dying process becomes the most significant passage of their lives. Theirs is a hereafter of more joy than they can possibly imagine.

God Knows You Have Value in the Here and Now

I once cornered Dr. J. I. Packer, a prominent evangelical theologian, and asked him this question. "What would you suggest to a severely handicapped man with cerebral palsy who was totally bedridden, nonverbal, and relegated to a back bedroom in a nursing home? No one visits him and no nurse takes time to benefit from his good attitude. What can that handicapped man do?" I knew plenty of real-life examples, so the question wasn't hypothetical.

Dr. Packer folded his hands, thought for a moment, and then replied, "A man like that can worship and glorify God."

That response almost sounded as though Dr.

Packer were piously patting the handicapped man on the head and trivializing his plight with a platitude that was too heavenly minded. But I've encountered enough handicapped people, just like the man with cerebral palsy, to know that Dr. Packer is right, and I've looked long enough into the Bible to know his advice is well taken.

I think of Tracy Traylor, a beautiful blonde-haired college student who suffered a severe head injury and was in a coma for five and one-half months. She came out of it unable to walk or talk well enough for people outside her family to understand her.

I met Tracy and her mother at a conference. Tracy, sitting slumped in her wheelchair, slightly lifted her bobbing head and shoved something in her lap toward me. It was a necklace made of clay and colored beads, and one of the clay pieces had an imprint of a leaping deer.

"Oh Tracy," I said, "this is beautiful. Thank you for the gift."

"My daughter was a design student in college and she directs me on how to craft each piece of jewelry," her mother proudly explained. I could hardly imagine the enormous effort it took for the two of them to communicate.

Just then I noticed a verse typed on a piece of paper twist-tied to the necklace. It was Isaiah 35:4, 6, "Your God will come . . . Then will the lame leap like a deer." I couldn't hold back the tears. Although Tracy couldn't speak, her smile spoke volumes. Her brilliant and shining hope cast shadows on me. I glanced around at the hundreds of people who were rushing by us, each of them oblivious to the powerful message of the college girl in her wheelchair.

Maybe millions of people could care less about this girl's lovely attitude, but Someone far more significant cared, and He had a purpose. "The purpose is that all the angelic powers should now see the complex wisdom of God's plan being worked out through the church."[16]

Whether a godly attitude shines from a brain-injured college student or from a lonely man relegated to a back bedroom, the response of patience and perseverance counts. God points to the peaceful attitude of suffering people to teach others about Himself. He not only teaches those we rub shoulders with every day, but He instructs the countless millions of angels and demons. The hosts in heaven stand amazed when they observe God sustain hurting people with His peace.

It matters to God not only *that* you live but *how* you live.

God Can Be Trusted Even When There Are No Reasons

The message was scribbled and rain splattered: "Laurel Ledford needs to talk to you." We met in an office at the retreat center where I was speaking. I was surprised when she entered the room carrying her three-month-old baby. It was cold and windy, not the kind of day you would take an infant outside. But then again it wasn't easy for Laurel to find someone to baby-sit her son with spina bifida. She sat across from me in a heavy sweater, holding her handicapped child bundled in blankets.

Laurel relayed her story, one incident after another of heart-twisting disappointment. First they moved after selling all they had so her husband, Steve, could go to school. Then they had one child named Stephen. Next she carried and lost a baby girl. Then another. Immediately after the loss of her second child, she accidentally became pregnant. When she was six months along, her husband had surgery, which further drained their already limited bank account.

She tugged at her little boy's blanket and in tears, said, "I thought I could handle losing another baby, but I could definitely not handle a baby with a birth defect. Shortly after that, my doctor told me that the baby I was carrying had severe hydrocephalus and spina bifida. He told me that one option would be to have a spontaneous delivery."

"You mean abortion?"

Laurel nodded. I mentally added the phrase "spontaneous delivery" to that list of pleasant-sounding euphemisms.

"But I would *not* choose to lose my baby," she said. "Still that's when depression and thoughts of suicide came to mind. I spent a long, gray midwestern winter on the couch watching a lot of TV."

Laurel went on to say that after the birth of

David, her baby with spina bifida, she struggled with more feelings of hopelessness. "David's head size looked terrible, and I was struggling with bonding. I didn't want him or even like him. I had so much guilt and confusion—"

I had to interrupt. "What kept you going?"

Laurel hiked David on her lap to think. "I plastered our walls with Scriptures. Psalm 34 says, 'The Lord is close to the brokenhearted and saves those who are crushed in spirit.'" Then she paused for another long moment. "But sometimes I still get so depressed. There's no rhyme or reason for why all these awful things have happened."

She had a point. Any information I might have given Laurel at that moment would have come off sounding like clichés; sometimes the magnitude of a person's suffering seems to outweigh any potential benefit. The puzzle of suffering doesn't always get completed. There are sometimes no reasons that satisfy. As Laurel pressed her lips to the bulging forehead of little David, I thought of a verse from Deuteronomy 29:29, "The secret things belong to the Lord our God."

"Joni," Laurel said, startling me from my thoughts. "How do I face tomorrow?" Her liquid brown eyes looked so pleading.

I took a deep breath. "I have to confess I wonder the same thing. I get weak-kneed thinking about living another twenty-five years in a wheelchair. But God does not expect me to accept what may or may not happen to me twenty years from now."

Laurel gave a questioning look.

"God doesn't give strength to face next year's headaches or even next month's heartaches. He won't even loan you enough strength to face tomorrow. He only gives you and I strength to face today. To live one day at a time."

She nodded, as if understanding.

"I'm sure that's why Jesus said, 'Do not worry about tomorrow, for tomorrow will worry about itself. Each day has enough trouble of its own.'[17] You'll have to face tomorrow, Laurel, without answers to your questions. The best you and I can do is hold onto the One who holds the answers."

We spent the rest of our time together in silence, mostly listening to David breathe softly and sigh every once in a while. We both sensed that enough words had been spoken. Yet in the quiet a bond was growing between us. After a while, we hugged and said good-bye.

A month or so later I received a letter from Laurel. Life had not gotten easier. One evening Stephen, her older boy, disappeared. She was sick with panic. Neighbors were telephoned, the police were contacted, a search began. When Laurel heard the patrol car calling in the K-9 unit, she fell apart. "It was as if a demon were screaming into my ears, 'Do it now! Kill yourself! Shove your wrists through the front window!'"

A half hour later her son was found. He had been hiding in the house the whole time.

Why? What reasons could there possibly be for

the torment and pain? There's no answer. But I noticed a P.S. at the close of her letter, a message that was better than any answer: "I'm trying to reach out to at least one person a day and do something for them that counts for eternity. It works!"

Your Decision Matters to a Personal God

Laurel heard the devil screeching in her ear one moment and God whispering in her other ear the next. Should she shut her ears to the devil's lies, or against God's words? Laurel teeters almost daily on the edge of eternity—that's why she sees every day as a choice. And her decision goes far beyond whether or not she should "Do it! Do it! End your life!"

Laurel, and many like her who have been tempted to leapfrog all the suffering, grit their teeth and decide daily to live. For these friends, life has value now and value in the hereafter.

It's something they remind themselves of each day. It's a decision they act on, a decision that matters to God.

PART THREE

A Time to Die

8

Sustaining Life But Not Prolonging Death

My father should have been raised as a cowboy on the open plains. Actually he almost was. Born in 1900, he led a rough-rider life, trading with Indians in the Northwest and scaling the highest peaks of the Rockies. I loved following in his footsteps, riding fast horses, hiking high mountains, and camping under the moon and stars. Dad was my hero.

When I was little, he took me and my sisters to see a movie about Eskimos called *The Young Savages*. I was troubled by a scene in which an elderly Eskimo who was dying was left behind on an ice floe. We talked about it on the way home, and although I can't remember my father's words, I knew that Daddy would probably have chosen the same path.

I forgot about that movie until decades later when my father became physically and mentally debilitated by a series of strokes that left him virtually bedridden. It was the long-feared nightmare that we, while growing up, always pushed from our minds.

Our ninety-year-old dad was but a shadow of his former self. His withered, bony frame couldn't hide the undaunted spirit that twinkled from his blue eyes, and it crushed our hearts to think that Daddy was probably going to die within a year, maybe months, or even weeks.

The family house in Maryland was sold. Mother moved her and Dad to Florida where he resided in a cheery, little nursing home. Mom walked from my uncle's house to the nursing home every morning to care for her husband's needs and then returned at night after he was put to bed. My sisters and I often visited, and Linda, Jay, and Kathy most frequently stretched their visits so they could help our mother and dad.

Then, in a span of less than two weeks, everything changed. My father began to quickly fail. He was rushed to the hospital. An IV was inserted. The tube was later removed when his body bloated and lungs filled. He was sent back to the nursing home. Our family collapsed in exhaustion. We agonized and conferred with doctors. After much prayer and painful discussion, we made a decision: no feeding tube. It was clear Daddy was dying, and knowing my father, he would not want the process of his dying prolonged. My sisters and mom tenderly cared for Daddy around the clock during his last days, camping on couch pillows by his bedside and giving him what little water he could take.

Within days I received a phone call from Jay.

Daddy had passed away. I sat for a long moment and then put my thoughts on paper.

> In that little nursing home, my mother had sat vigil with Dad for over a year and a half, helping him daily and spreading the joy of the Lord to every elderly person up and down each hallway. In this last week, I joined my sisters and Mom there. It was obvious Dad was failing fast.
>
> I had to leave after a few days—it was a tearful departure, knowing I'd never see my father again this side of eternity. But now, just days later, they called to say how Dad had turned to my mother, opened both his blue eyes for the first time in days, gave her a big, full smile and languished for a moment in what they emphatically described as a "glow." It must have been the glow of God's presence because then . . . he passed away.
>
> My mother, sisters, a recreational therapist, and a nurse held hands around his bed and sang a doxology. From there, my sisters canvassed the hallways telling people, "Daddy just went to heaven to be with the Lord . . . isn't that exciting?"

When It Comes to Dying, We Need the Wisdom of God

Who would have dreamed the day would come when the family of a dying loved one would have to study a medical dictionary to discern exactly what "dying" was. We all wish dying were as easy to read as "Naked I came from my mother's womb, and naked I will depart. The Lord gave and the Lord has taken away."[1]

It seems simple. God gives life, God takes life away, and there's a line between the two. But where is the line? Has modern technology thrown a monkey wrench into the way God gives and takes life? Has modern medicine presented Him with problems to which even He has no answer?

If God has given man tools with which to sustain life, it would seem impossible to outrun His wisdom. God, by nature, can't say, "Well, people, I don't know what to do about those machines and treatments you've invented. They're new to me. You'll have to make those decisions in your realm because I can't comprehend it all, much less offer wisdom."

God doesn't operate that way. If He provides man with the talent to advance and invent on behalf of life, He must also provide the wisdom to make decisions. And the question begging wisdom is this: *What is the distinction between providing a person with all the life to which he's entitled as opposed to artificially prolonging the process of his death*?

Most of us wish that someone else would do the moral choosing for us, just explaining flat-out the differences. Some people look for wisdom by polling the majority, asking what "most people" would do. Others go with their gut feelings, ranging in degree of certainty from "I think I know what's best but don't ask me to explain it" to "I'm absolutely right about this." Many people rely on their conscience, which is a little better than going by feelings, but it still falls short. None of these is reliable because feelings vary, the majority is often wrong, and an armor of conscience is only as dependable as its weakest piece. There must be a better place to find wisdom.

God Gives Necessary Wisdom for a Particular Problem

The Bible is full of God's wisdom. And from it we can derive wisdom—that is, the power of judging the soundest course of action based on knowledge and experience.[2]

First, there are definite "do's" and "don'ts" in Scripture. "Thou shalt not murder" is pretty straightforward. However, when there are no Scriptural commands, you're forced to look closer. Some actions are commendable, some are permitted, and some are prohibited by Scripture. The Bible is a big book and it takes a little research to decipher between the "don't do's" and the "maybe do's."

Second, since the Bible is a book to be applied in practical living, we next need to consider the many different situations that a person can face today. Use of a respirator may be good in one situation, bad in another. Kidney dialysis may be appropriate for one person but not the next. Chemotherapy may be great for some but wrong for others. Radical amputation may be considered an ordinary procedure on a seventeen-year-old diabetic girl, but on a ninety-year-old man struggling with diabetes it may be futile and burdensome.

Once we have considered these situations, we need to understand what Scripture says about a particular situation to determine what is morally right.

So let's go back to the example of the respirator. It may look easy to unhook a life support, but Scripture demands that we examine our judgment through the lens of God's Word. Look closely: Scripture says that life is precious. That suffering people should have every access to God's grace. That love for God and love for others is paramount. That motives are important. That conscience cannot be violated. And so on.

These guidelines, and others from Scripture, have a powerful bearing on whether or not we are free to pull the plug. They should guide in every situation, eliminating slipshod ethics and "tragic moral choices."

That's what wisdom is all about: employing knowledge and experience to judge the soundest course of action, right? Right. And when my family sought wisdom for Dad's situation, it was helpful to be able to reach for a verse from the shelf of theory and use it in the hospital ward where our decisions had to be made.

A good word on wisdom is James 1:5: "If any of you does not know how to meet a *particular problem* he has only to ask God . . . and he may be quite sure that the *necessary wisdom* will be given him. But he must ask in sincere faith without any secret doubts" (TLB).

Right there God supplies almost half the answer for our need. Like the verse says, He promises He'll give *necessary* wisdom to a *particular* problem— that is, wisdom tailored to the problem at hand. Custom-fitted wisdom is needed for discerning particular life or dying distinctions. And because it involves the life and death of a warm-blooded human being, each distinction is subjective, definitely not objective. Every situation is different, every person is unique.

So when it comes to the "pull the plug" question, don't waste your time looking for rules one-two-three and a tidy list of do's and don'ts. My family couldn't superimpose on Dad the experience of other families in that nursing home. In the same way, you can't take my family's decision and overlay it like a template on your family's situation. It doesn't work that way. Even Dr. C. Everett Koop, the former Surgeon General has said, "There is no way that there can be a set of rules to govern this circumstance. Guidelines may be possible, but not rules."[3]

Yet don't be overwhelmed and throw your hands up in despair. Your process of making personal decisions is as close as your doctor, family, and clergy. Insight for making distinctions can be drawn from the experience of a caring physician, the condition of the dying person, and the input of the family and religious counselors. Historically, life-and-death decisions have always been made this way. "Safety is found in the abundance of counselors" and wisdom is gathered from a physician who knows the facts, a patient who has expressed his wishes, a family who is looking out for their loved one first and foremost, and a pastor who can give godly guidance.[4]

A good relationship between physician, patient, family, and pastor can be the wellspring of wisdom. But underline the word relationship. Unfortunately the care, trust, and confidence that once earmarked the fraternity between a doctor and the patient and a family has been replaced by new industry standards. The doctor has now become a health-care provider who offers a paid service to us, the consumers. It's rare to find physicians and families that build their relationship on trust, time, and commitment. And trust, plus an up-close and personal relationship is needed to discern what is best for a dying family member.

If you feel that your physician only relates to you on a paid-for-service basis, then it may be time to change doctors.

Wisdom in the Life-and-Death Setting

Also, James 1:5 implies that a lot of wisdom is already revealed. Remember those commands? The obvious do's and don'ts? Life is a good and God-given thing; it is the most fundamental and irreplaceable condition of the human experience. God is the first one who said, "Choose life," so it's always wise to go ahead and choose those directives that would be life beneficial to a person.[5]

But is it wise to pump up a person who is in the final death throes with more treatments and machines? Of course not. Dying begins when a person rapidly and irreversibly deteriorates, a person for whom death is imminent, a person who is beyond reasonable hope of recovery. Such people have a right to not have death postponed.[6]

The line of distinction is not so much between life and death, as it is between life and dying. There are pages in medical dictionaries devoted to defining imminent death. But because the people who are "imminently dying" are unique warm-blooded human beings in unique circumstances, it's impossible to pin down exactly when the process of dying begins. The International Anti-Euthanasia Task Force says that true imminent death spans a period of days, perhaps hours. However, courts in some states widen the span of imminent death to a matter of weeks, and some say months! That's why a good relationship with your family's doctors is so critical. You need to get as close to the facts as possible.

There's a point, though, when it's futile and even burdensome to go into a full-court press against death using every last bit of high-tech heroic treatment available. Dr. Koop advises,

> If someone is dying and there is no doubt about that, and you believe as I do that there is a difference between giving a person all the life to which he is entitled as opposed to prolonging the

act of dying, then you might come to a time when you say this person can take certain amounts of fluid by mouth and we're not going to continue this intravenous solution because he is on the way out.[7]

This is what "death with dignity" is supposed to be all about.

Okay, so it's possible to gain wisdom about life and dying distinctions. Now what do we do with that wisdom? James 1:5 goes so far as to warn us against asking for wisdom while holding onto secret doubts. It is over this point so many people stumble.

God demands that we examine our motives. Some people may secretly want a loved one to die to relieve the family's suffering, or for economic considerations, or perhaps even out of convenience to the caregivers or society. Think back to what Dr. Koop said, "The whole thing about euthanasia comes down to one word: motive." If family members insist that IV's and tubes be withheld or withdrawn because "Dad's best years are being wasted taking care of Mother," or "They left that nest egg for us, not for paying hospital bills," then secret doubts could take precedence over God's wisdom.

What About Life-Support Systems?

The passing away of my father taught my family about finding wisdom in helping my dad live and letting him die. Giving food to the hungry and water to the thirsty is a requirement of basic decency. And even when it was clear my father had entered that irrevocable process of death, we wanted to make him as comfortable as possible. This is part of the revealed wisdom of God that mandates compassionate care. It's one of those Scriptural "do's."

However, doctors advised my family that there are situations where giving food or water, whether by mouth or by tube feeding, is futile and excessively burdensome. Rita Marker of the International Anti-Euthanasia Task Force says,

> A patient who is very close to death may be in such a condition that fluids would cause a great deal of discomfort or may not be assimilated by his body. Food may not be digested as the body begins "shutting down" during the dying process. There comes a time when a person is truly, imminently dying.[8]

The Christian Medical Society affirms that, "in exceptional cases, tube feeding may actually result in increased patient suffering during the dying process."[9]

My father was one example—had he tolerated better the intravenous tube, had he not been dying, we would have faced a different set of circumstances. But we as a family knew his wants and wishes; we knew the way he would want to die. We had asked ourselves the important questions: Were we certain Dad had begun to actually die? Were our motives pure? Our conscience clear? Did we thoroughly seek the counsel of our doctor and clergy? Were we convinced of God's will in this situation?

And most important, were we sure of Dad's salvation in Jesus Christ?

Yes. Yes, to all those questions. And basic decency was lived out poignantly as Kathy, Jay, and my mother moistened Dad's lips with ice chips, helped him sip juice when he was able, and even clear broth when possible.

By the way, had my father needed massive pain medication, our family and doctors would have done whatever was necessary to make him comfortable. As it was, my father was comfortable without medication, but Proverbs 31:6–7 makes a strong case for strong analgesics, "Give beer to those who are perishing, wine to those who are in anguish; let them drink and forget their poverty and remember their misery no more." In the context of Proverbs, wine is a bad and deceitful thing, but in these two verses, its anesthetic and analgesic qualities are commendable for those who are dying or "in anguish."

These are the decisions we made based on an understanding of *Scripture* and my dying father's *situation*. But what about the families of people in comas or persistent vegetative states? What about their artificial life-support systems? What about the medical treatment and basic care of people who are severely disabled to the point where the line between life and death is drawn by a respirator?

These are questions that would test even wise King Solomon himself!

The Person With a Disability

Dan Piantine is not dying, he's a young man in his early twenties who is disabled. The first time Dan and I bumped wheelchairs, I was taken aback by the severity of his paralysis and his frail, thin body. Dan was born with a neuromuscular disease and thus never developed good muscles. Some people have said he'd be better off dead than disabled. But Dan is full of life and it troubles me when they say that he's suffering needlessly or that he's imprisoned by his body. Such phrases purport to be compassionate but reveal a fundamental fear that really says "I'd hate to live like that."

For our brief time together, we forgot about such people. Dan and I laughed and talked about our dreams, hopes, and God.

The second time I met with Dan, it was on a rainy, windy afternoon as he was resting inside his transparent iron lung—a recent heart attack had forced him to spend more time lying down. Through the plastic cylinder I could see how scoliosis had severely bent and twisted his small body. I positioned my chair so I could watch his face in the mirror above the iron lung; I could also see when the whooshing vacuum caused his small, fragile frame to rise and fall. The rain pattered against the window and the feeling inside his room was quiet and relaxed.

"Joni, there was a time when I thought I'd be better off dead. I pondered the thought of removing myself from my life-support. Funny thing is, I don't think of my iron lung as a life support because there are no tubes, wires, or nurses needed. And my 'lung' is not what they call extraordinary care. For me it's ordinary. Just something to help me breathe like, let's say, somebody who has polio."

I knew what Dan was saying. What he was describing was *necessary* wisdom needed for his *particular* situation. What is "extraordinary" care for some people is plain "ordinary" for others. Every person is different, each circumstance unique.

Dan continued, "But God showed me that the definition of quality of life was wrapped up in carrying out His will for my life. No matter what my situation, God could use me."

"We're peas in a pod on that one," I laughed. I knew of Dan's intensive efforts to educate his religious denomination on accessibility. His heart was bursting with ideas and vision. His body, however, was slowing down. I thought about his recent heart attack and asked, "Have you thought about dying? How will you face it?"

"I've signed a living will stating that when my condition worsens and I can no longer be kept alive by an iron lung, I refuse to accept treatment in other forms. You see, the only other treatment would be a respirator requiring a tracheotomy. I've talked with doctors about this, and in assessing my condition," he said as his eyes gestured toward his body, "I feel a respirator would ultimately end in my death because I have so many physical difficulties. I could write a medical journal on my disease alone!"

He went on, "We've come so far in technology that the absolute of when life ends and death is imminent is no longer black and white. I don't want to be caught in the gray. Hey, I'm not saying I have the right to pull myself off my iron lung this minute any more than to ask a doctor to inject a lethal drug. But when it comes to one day facing the way I'll die . . ."

"You've made a judgment in advance," I quietly said. I wasn't going to debate his decision about using a different kind of respirator. Dan had obviously talked with his family and his pastor. He had had many discussions with his doctor. And although I know scores of severely disabled people who use trach-respirators and would vehemently argue that Dan should go for the "trach," I have to respect his decision.

Why? Because Dan understands Scripture, he understands his situation, and he has worked through the process of making this incredibly important decision. I have to respect Dan's choice because . . .

—He's *mentally competent* and by no means suicidal. That means he has the *legal right* to decline treatment.

—His *motive* in refusing the trach is not to hurry on his death, but safeguard his best chances for life.

—He's conferred with his doctor, is a disability

expert, and is *totally informed* about his condition. He has weighed the risks.

—He has *specifically expressed* his wishes, underscoring that further treatment would be extraordinary and burdensome.

—And as a *Christian*, Dan is heading for heaven.

When I left Dan's room that day it was still gray and windy. The dark afternoon made me wonder about the way I would approach death as a quadriplegic. Like Dan I'm an expert on my disability—spinal cord injury has left me severely disabled, but nowhere near to the extent as Dan. Knowing my kind of quadriplegia, a trach-respirator would definitely *not* be burdensome if, let's say, it got me through pneumonia. And even if I became permanently dependent on a respirator as a result of pneumonia, it would not be excessively burdensome or futile treatment. Goodness, a respirator would provide significant life benefits! Not so for Dan because a respirator could bring on serious and life-threatening complications.

So if I decline a respirator, it would be the same as committing suicide. Even though we're both severely disabled, it's obvious my circumstances are different from Dan's. There are no black-and-white rules that force us to the same decision.

Thus the question: When is artificial life support extraordinary and when is it ordinary? Treatment that significantly sustains life in a beneficial way is ordinary. Treatment that merely postpones or prolongs the act of dying could be considered extraordinary. When I look at my debilitated friends who are on respirators, dialysis machines, or iron lungs, it's clear such assistive devices are very ordinary treatment. Respirators, "lungs," and even a catheter for someone like me produce significant life benefits in relation to the discomfort and cost.

But a respirator, or a dialysis machine, or even extensive, expensive surgery could easily be considered extraordinary or burdensome treatment on others. Assistive devices in some cases could be uncomfortable, costly, and result in no significant life benefits. It's another one of those subjective distinctions.

I appreciate the way Dr. C. Everett Koop reasons:

> Right now, I am seventy years old and in excellent health. If my kidneys shut down tomorrow, let's say, after a severe infection, I don't know how long I would want to be on dialysis. It would be foolish and a waste of resources for me to have a kidney transplant at my age. I would probably opt to clean up my affairs, say goodbye to my family, and drift out in uremia. The point is that my wife and I know exactly how each of us feels about the end of life— this will be crucial if the time comes to make such a decision and I'm not then able to do so.[10]

The guidelines that steer a person with a handicapping condition through the maze of life-and-death questions are very much the same for the person who is terminally ill. A man with AIDS, or a woman with cancer, or a child with cystic fibrosis all may be at points in their lives where, like Dan, they are living just fine with ordinary treatment. But, like him, one day their condition will deteriorate. They too will wonder, "My doctors say I only have several months to live. Is it worth having that major surgery?" These people will try their best to stay out of the gray areas of life-and-death decisions. They will need necessary wisdom for their particular situations.

They will need the wisdom of James 1:5.

The Person in a Coma or Persistent Vegetative State

Sometimes letters say it all. Like this one from the mother of a boy named Jeremy:

Dear Joni,

Our twelve-year-old child, Jeremy, was critically injured in an automobile accident in 1986. He lived but remained in a comatose state—we later learned that Jeremy was in a "locked in" condition, unable to open his eyes or speak. He was well nourished through a feeding tube.

We didn't think we could communicate with Jeremy. But after two years of hard work, physical therapy, God's grace and money, one day it happened. When I put a softball under his hand, he very slightly moved his thumb for "yes" and his little finger for "no." Our precious son suffered much during two and one-half years and then the Lord took him home shortly before his fifteenth birthday. God used Jeremy's dark valley to point others to him.

Patty Cabeen

Stories like Jeremy's are baffling. Is he in a coma? A state of permanent unconsciousness? Then there's the term persistent vegetative state (PVS). Add to that, the doctor's assessment that Jeremy was in a "locked-in condition." To clear up the confusion, a person in a coma is in a suspended sleep state from which he may or may not awaken. A person in a persistent vegetative state is awake, has sleep cycles but almost always cannot relate to those around them. Patty's son, with a slight move of his thumb and little finger, was able to connect with those around him and that's why his condition was termed "locked in."

Jeremy's story is at once inspiring yet sad. He represents thousands who are in permanent comas or vegetative states. Many of these are said to be hopelessly beyond recovery. Ultimately that means they are in danger of losing personhood (and all the rights that go with being a person, including the right to life).

It is precisely these people in permanent comas or in PVS around which the right-to-die debate is really raging. These are the ones most at risk, these are the ones who are in danger of losing their lives. "The persistent vegetative state is being used as the hard case in order to get people used to the idea that there are some in our society whose lives aren't worthwhile, who can be terminated," says Dr. William Burke, a professor of neurology at St. Louis University.[11]

People in comas or PVS are the ones who, more

often than not, have never made clear their wishes about respirators or feeding tubes. And their families are the ones most burdened and distressed. We can hardly imagine the pain, the financial crunch, the tears, trauma, and heartache they must endure.

These mothers and fathers, and husbands or wives, are placed in the awkward position of speaking on behalf of the person in PVS or a coma. And often, health-care professionals and the courts veto the family's directives. There are even cases where the family vetos the doctor's directives, and the courts veto everybody's directives!

The question is usually: Why can't we let this person die?

It is at this exact point that I firmly pull on my hat as a disability advocate. People in comas or persistent vegetative states or even locked-in conditions, much like Jeremy's, aren't dying (although Jeremy eventually died of complications); they are severely disabled. Sure, underline the word severely because some of these people can't swallow, others can. Some make movements that are intentional, others reflexive. Because they are nonverbal, they depend on the sensitive interpretations of their caregivers, just as the mother of a newborn can sense differences in a whimper. And some even dramatically recover after spending years in a coma or vegetative state.

But all things considered, they are disabled. They just happen to be more incapacitated than even someone like Dan. And people, no matter how severe their handicapping condition, are entitled to treatment and care. Perhaps their biggest handicap is that they are "socially disabled," unable to relate to people around them. They are further socially disabled because public sentiment is most often behind their stressed-out families. But people like Jeremy are still persons. And each one has a soul, a spirit.

I won't take time to elaborate on the right-to-die debate swirling around these people and their parents, husbands, or wives, since others have written exhaustively on it. But there is one perspective about an individual in a long-term coma or PVS that I rarely hear: The Spirit of God is able to work dramatically in the spirit of such a person, perhaps more so than at any other time in his life.

It may appear that nothing is taking place in the life of a man or woman in a coma or vegetative state, but remember that the work of God is spiritual activity, often very separate from a person's intellect or even basic brain activity. I know of people who have lain in bed for years, unable to relate. I also know of friends or family members who have sat at their bedsides and prayed, read Scripture or poetry, played inspirational music, laughed and loved with them. And I know that many of these people have come out of their sleep having connected with God in an extraordinary way.

How does that happen? Jesus said, "[Spiritual revelations] are not revealed to you by man, but by my Father in heaven."[12] And God can definitely work in the lives of people who have no intellectual capacity. Just look at the example of John the Baptist. While he was yet in his mother's womb, he leaped for joy. And even at his birth, he was filled with the Holy Spirit.[13] Obviously, God did not need the brain of that baby in order to make Himself known. What a profound thought: God may not require a mind through which to reveal Himself!

This is good news for people who don't have a high IQ. It's good news for the child or adult who is mentally retarded. And this is probably the only, and best, good news for the more than ten thousand people in this country who are in comatose states. I'm convinced God does not need their brains, whether injured or traumatized, to reveal His truth.

And what happens when that time comes for the person in a coma or PVS to depart this earth? How can a family member rest in the knowledge that their loved one has made that right turn into heaven? As Dr. John Frame of Westminster Theological Seminary concludes, "You simply commend the person to God's mercy. Can a person be saved by God's grace in the moments of unconsciousness preceding death? Certainly."[14]

Admittedly a truckload of arguments for "pulling the plugs" of respirators or feeding tubes can be stockpiled against the needs of people in comas or vegetative states: medical expenses, quality of life, family stress, patient suffering, the precedence of court rulings, and the pressure from the public. But it is for these very reasons that we should "Stop evaluating by what the world thinks about them or by what they seem to be like on the outside," as it says in 2 Corinthians 5:16 (TLB).

Such arguments, convincing as they may be, may dictate that it's reasonable to remove life-support systems—in spite of the fact that to do so would be active euthanasia. Rather, people like Jeremy need to be regarded from a transcendent and eternal view. "For what is seen is temporary, but what is unseen is eternal."[15]

That's Fine for Jeremy, But ...

Let's be honest. Maybe you could never see yourself facing life as Jeremy did. You could never live like that. You have enormous respect for Patty Cabeen and her son, but personally, you just would not want to live in permanent unconsciousness or in a persistent vegetative state. You want some kind of control over what happens to you.

For you there is also another kind of answer.

9

Knowing the Difference Isn't Easy

If I expect life to be unending, then dying seems to
be an illusion. If I live life as a vocation, then dying
is an intrusion. If life is a threat, then dying is an
escape. If I accept life as a gift, then dying is a part of
the given.[1]

Ben Coombs, an estate planner and a friend from
my church, pulled up a chair next to my desk,
opened his briefcase, and spread before me a four-
page form titled "Durable Power of Attorney for
Health-Care Decisions." It explained how to ap-
point someone to make health-care decisions if I
became unable to decide for myself. My eyes slowly
scanned each intimidating page. As I zeroed in on
one part of the form, the part that looked a little like
a living will, the language seemed especially off-
putting.

Under number four, Statement of Desires, it read:

I want my life to be prolonged and I want life-
sustaining treatment to be provided unless I am in a
coma that my doctors reasonably believe to be
irreversible. Once my doctors have reasonably concluded I am in an irreversible coma, I do not want

life-sustaining treatment to be provided or continued.

I nervously bit my lip and read the paragraph again. The column next to it went even further. It talked about withholding or withdrawing life-sustaining procedures altogether. But then I glanced at the next column, which presented a dramatic alternative:

> I want my life to be prolonged to the greatest extent possible without any regard to my condition, the chances I have for recovery or the costs of the procedures.[2]

I squirmed a little in my wheelchair. "Why do I have to sign this section?" I asked. "Can't my husband just privately tell the doctors my views on prolonged treatment?" Ben pointed out that the person whom I would legally select to make health-care decisions for me—if I was unable to make those decisions for myself—needed to faithfully represent my known wishes.

I looked at the place where I would date, sign, and have the form notarized. "What if I change my mind?"

"You should update this every seven years, Joni. Unfortunately," Ben said as he shrugged his shoulders and flipped over the document, "not many people even know about designating a health-care proxy. What few do, keep putting it off. Then there are those who never take the time to keep the document up to date." He shook his head and paused for a moment. "A lot of headache and heartache could be avoided if people only took time to prepare for the future."

I knew exactly what he meant. The physical setbacks I had suffered in 1991 forced me to think about the way I wanted to approach my own process of dying. I needed to prayerfully and carefully think through health-care decisions, especially if, in the future, I was mentally unable to think.

Questions to Consider

Before I signed my "Joni Tada" on any dotted line, there were serious questions I had to ask. The first was straight out of Psalm 39, "Show me, O Lord, my life's end and the number of my days." *On one hand, Lord, You say that "length of days" is a blessing, but there has to be a "time to die."*³ *This is no decision I can make in a vacuum, it has to involve the Lord and Giver of my life. I need to know what You think about the choices facing me.*

It helped that I already had an other-worldly perspective on the process of death. The apostle Paul, who was near death himself, was able to confidently say, "We . . . would prefer to be away from the body and at home with the Lord. So we make it our goal to please him, whether we are at home in the body or away from it."⁴ I wanted my decision about the way I would die to meet with His approval, from the last breath I would draw on this side of eternity, to the split-second I crossed the line to the other side.

My decision also involved more than God and me. There were others to consider. For my family's sake it was important to leave an advance directive about the sort of death I wanted to face. To not sign the document about a health-care proxy could place my husband Ken in an awkward position, especially if I were unconscious or mentally incompetent. If a hospital or the state took issue with Ken's directives about my care, then under the judicial doctrine of "substituted judgment," the court would assume the responsibility of determining my desires regarding medical treatment. Without having documented evidence of my wants and wishes, Ken might end up in a fight with the courts over my almost-dead body.

Also I needed to assess my relationship with Ken, my family, friends, and associates. How would my choices in dying affect them? Would any of my decisions cause intolerable guilt or stress for my husband? And I needed to cement my relationship with my doctor. Did we both appreciate the limitations of my disability? Did I understand all the facts about life-support systems and their help or hindrance to me?

Having thought through these questions and more, I decided to sign the Durable Power of Attorney for Health Care, for my family's sake, for my protection, and for God's commendation.

I took the document home for Ken to study. He

knew I had wanted to designate him, and an alternate proxy, as my health-care agents, but we had been putting off the discussion for some time. After dinner, Ken opened the folder on the kitchen table and slowly read each section. He was quiet and I wondered what he was thinking.

Much later in the evening, he came into the bedroom and sat on the edge of our bed. "This is a good thing to do," he sighed. "A little difficult to talk about, but a good thing." He looked straight at me and said, "Well, what have you decided?"

"I know my body better than anybody," I said, "and I know that twenty-five years of paralysis have taken their toll. Let's say when I'm a little older I face heart failure, or need to have a kidney removed or maybe go on dialysis. Quadriplegia has already caused poor circulation and has put my kidneys in jeopardy, so I just don't think it would be worth the risk. I'd probably opt not to have major surgery. Do you see what I mean?"

Ken nodded.

"Plus, I was reading in the Bible the other day about receiving a new body when I get to heaven. That alone makes me not afraid of death," I said. "Like it says, 'And we eagerly await a Savior . . . the Lord Jesus Christ who . . . will transform our lowly bodies so that they will be like his glorious body.' "[5]

"You sound like a walking theology textbook," he said.

"Listen, if you were paralyzed for as long as me, you'd be excited about getting a body that worked, too," I said with a smile. "Anyway, like I mentioned, I'm not afraid of death, but with things so high-tech, and with hospitals so . . . so mechanistic, I'm a little afraid of the way I could die."

"And this is why you want us to sign this," Ken said as he tapped the document in his hand. I nodded and we both sat there for a long moment. The rest of the evening we spent discussing our wants and wishes of "in sickness and in health, 'til death do us part."

A Living Will Versus a Durable Power of Attorney for Health Care

Why would I designate a health-care proxy? Why not simply sign a living will? At first glance the living will sounds good. You have the chance to write down on paper exactly how "extraordinary" you want extraordinary medical treatment to be. But living wills have problems.

First, such documents send a signal that you don't want to have anything done. For instance, in a crowded emergency room, the overworked doctors on duty could interpret a living will to mean that you do not want to be resuscitated, period. Your stretcher is shoved against a wall while other emergencies waiting in line are ushered in.

Second, a living will can't be erased at the last minute. You have no idea when you write it what sort of death you will face, or what sort of new treatments may become available. There's simply no way you can accurately foresee the details. And who knows, you may like most people want to change your mind when faced with the fact of your own death.

People tend to think that a living will gives them control over the way they will die. But in fact, when you sign a living will, you give up rights and control to any doctor who happens to be on the scene to decipher it. There's no guarantee that your favorite friendly physician will be the one interpreting the vague wording of a living will.

"But," I hear you saying, "can't my family member explain to the doctor what I meant?"

True, family members can take a stab at deciphering what you meant and explaining it to the physicians on the scene, but the doctor doesn't have to heed the advice. The law gives complete power and protection to the physician who has the document in his hands. If it's your own doctor, there may not be a problem; but there's no guarantee that you'll be in the same hometown as your family physician when you sustain a serious injury or illness.

So which is it? Living wills or a designated proxy? It boils down to this: Do you want to be represented by a piece of paper or a person?

I want a person to speak for me. A person, unlike a living will, is flexible and can be responsive to the circumstances. A person can hire or fire a doctor or even discharge a patient from a hospital. But that individual had better know my exact wishes inside and out—my life would be in his hands! Of course, that brings me back to Ken and the Durable Power of Attorney for Health Care. I trust Ken, we share the same beliefs, and he knows me better than anybody. I want him to speak for me.

To be honest, neither living wills nor designated health proxies are perfect answers to the dilemma of dying, but of the two, the power of attorney holds sway. Yet, even appointing a person to make medical treatment decisions has its built-in problems. Laws vary all over the nation. One state excludes food and fluids from the category of life-sustaining procedures, and other states allow people to decide specifically whether or not they want food and water withheld.

What's the best thing to do? Ask questions. Whether in a family conference with the ethics committee at the hospital, or in a discussion with nurses and social workers, it's always good to ask.

The "Miranda" Law. You Have the Right to ...

Actually the Patient Self-Determination Act now requires hospitals or nursing homes that receive Medicare or Medicaid funds to explain which documents are recognized in your state, whether living wills or durable powers of attorney. Your rights as a patient are recited to you when you check into a hospital, a kind of detailed briefing like the Miranda warning that law officers give.

So, whether you're going in for major heart surgery or just overnight observation, you will be handed a frank written reminder of your right to refuse medical care should your condition become hopeless.

The law was originally drafted in response to the emotional and heartbreaking court proceedings over whether or not to withdraw life support, including food and water, from Nancy Cruzan, the young woman left in a comatose state after a terrible accident. The hope is that this Miranda-like law will make it far more likely that such problems will be resolved at the patient's bedside rather than in some distant courtroom. Nancy Cruzan, before her accident, had never written down her wishes about the way she would want to die. That's why there was so much controversy when her feeding tube was removed, not to mention the outrage that a young disabled woman was then starved to death.

In one sense the Patient Self-Determination Act is helpful because people need to know the facts. Yet in another sense it's alarming, even frightening. Just having a nurse confront you about living wills and then handing you a sheet spelling out your rights as you check into a hospital can be disconcerting. A question like that could affect your judgment about medical treatment, especially if you're depressed about being hospitalized. You wouldn't have any chance to think, pray, or plan wisely!

However, the Patient Self-Determination Act, for

all of its flaws, is an attempt to get people thinking about health-care proxies and living wills *before* illness strikes and rational thinking goes out the window.

So don't wait until you've checked into a hospital. Prayer is the key for preparing yourself and your family for your decision. Ask God to give you the necessary wisdom to make those important choices. Meet with your pastor. Talk with your spouse or parent. Find out from your doctor what directives are legal in your state, or ask your local hospital or senior citizens center to send you the information. If you wish, you can write to National Right to Life and request their document, "Will to Live." Then when you receive the information, don't put it off.

When You Sign on the Dotted Line

Okay. So I put my signature to a document. What about you?

Remember, a Durable Power of Attorney for Health Care is not only a legal directive, it is a moral directive as well. I'd advise you to review a couple of key moral issues before predetermining medical treatment.

If you were my personal friend and I knew that you were about to hammer in concrete "No life supports in case of emergency," I would say, "Wait! What if you only need those life supports for a few days? What if then you'd be fine? Don't risk throwing your life away!" One more thing. If you exercised your right to predetermine "no life supports, including feeding tubes," you most likely would be asking that you be starved to death, a decision for which you are held morally responsible before God.

A Good Death

If anyone ever died "right" it was Kelly, my five-year-old niece. The youngest of three children, she was the typical tomboy on the family farm. Her mother Linda, a hardworking single parent, had given her children a lot of responsibilities around the house and barn, and Kelly had become a strong, resourceful, and independent little girl.

One day Granddad noticed that Kelly was limping up the dirt road, slightly dragging her foot. My sister Linda took her to the hospital, and doctors discovered an enormous cancerous brain tumor. We were shocked and stunned. Surgery could only do so much, and within a month she was confined to a wheelchair. After a long hospital stay, the doctors suggested we take Kelly home to die.

Now there were two sets of wheels around the dinner table, my adult size and Kelly's miniature one. The entire family rallied to focus love and attention on Kelly as she grew weaker. Everyone tried to make her as comfortable as possible. As a result, it was amazing to see the change in this little girl—not so much the physical change, but the change in her spirit and attitude. No longer the stiff-lipped "I don't need help, I can do it myself" tomboy, she softened into the sweetest, happiest child we ever knew. She virtually memorized "Goldilocks and the Three Bears," wore out her cousin Kay at playing tea, and most of all, let her imagination run wild when it came to talking about heaven.

Kelly tired easily during those last few months and spent more and more time in bed. She seemed to have no fear of the dark, her disability, or death. One night I remember passing her dark bedroom and hearing her sing in a half-whisper, "Jesus loves me, this I know. . ."

Kelly taught us a lot about dying right. She talked glowingly of when she would eat ice cream cones with Jesus. She would ride bigger ponies, douse all the ketchup she wanted on her hamburgers, and maybe even talk to bears like Goldilocks. At one point when we were alone in her room, I looked at her in all seriousness and asked, "Kelly, when you see Jesus, will you please tell Him that I said 'Hi'? You won't forget?"

She smiled and nodded.

Earlier in the evening on the night Kelly died, she said to her mother, "Mommy, I want to go home."

"But you are home, honey," my sister tenderly told her.

"No, I want to go home with Jesus," she whispered hoarsely. Within several hours she was there. Kelly passed away surrounded in bed by her family, stuffed animals, and a suitcase packed with her jeans, dresses, and toys. Kelly died right and that fact alone did more to ease the heartache and pain of her passing than anything else.

Hospice Care

Three simple things her family did made Kelly's death good. First, her pain was kept under control and she was made as comfortable as possible. Second, the family was brought together. Kelly gave sisters, cousins, uncles, and grandparents a reason to unite, support, and care for one another. Third, Kelly remained a part of the community. Neighborhood children played board games at her bedside, Granddad endlessly read picture books to her, and harmony rang out as she weakly joined in family sing-alongs. She was in almost constant contact with loving people, who continually convinced her she was not alone or deserted in her time of need.

What happened in Kelly's case is very much what happens in a hospice setting. We practiced most of the principles you would find in an in-patient hospice—that is, a place where people go to die. But a good hospice is not in the business of dying, but of living right up to the end. There's nothing institutional about rooms that are filled with homey furniture, throw rugs, and paintings on the walls. You may even see a beagle, someone's family pet, ambling down the hallway.

Modern medicine will often handle death very poorly. A hospital will go to great lengths for the sake of a patient with a chance of recovery. But a dying patient who languishes in a bed, a bed that others could be using, is often an embarrassment. Sometimes in a busy, crowded hospital, people who are terminally ill and dying are very much alone.

To me it's unfortunate that so much attention and so many resources in our society are funneled into legalizing euthanasia while the hospice movement is struggling to stay alive. To be honest, in the United States you are unlikely to be offered a bed in a hospice facility since there are very few. In-patient hospices, most of which are run by religious organizations, are in desperate need of volunteers, money, and facilities.

As a result, in this country the emphasis is on in-home hospice, the sort of thing we managed with Kelly. In-home hospice would provide a trained nurse for several days or a week to give a stressed-out caregiver a break. Social Security will even pay for some of the expenses of such care. But the movement needs help. We would communicate a far more compassionate message to those who are terminally ill and dying if we focused our energies on helping people die right.

To die right. That's what it's all about. Unfortunately euthanasia has become a popular topic because people are led to believe that death by suicide or homicide is more dignified than dying naturally. True, there can be bad medical treatment administered at the end of a person's life, but there are good treatments, too, symbolized in hospice care. It's the answer to those who fear a death that has been robbed of dignity by bad medical treatment.

We can even help debilitated or terminally ill people live right. We can alleviate the hopelessness that drives debilitated people to despair by advocating attendant or respite care for stressed-out families. We can support the family with counseling, visitation, or financial aid. Living or dying can be a lonely, desperate time for a person who is terminally ill. Our society, especially the spiritual community, cannot cringe at the misery that needs mercy or shun the burden that requires bearing. We must be the Lord's hands and heart to those who hurt.

A Dying Breath

Death, no matter how we plan for it, is still the last outrage. But we can make dying as peaceable and serene as possible. You actually can go through death in peace, even serenity. It all depends on the way you view life.

If you believe that your earthly life will continue uninterrupted, then you will never be prepared for your final passage, no matter how many documents you sign.

If you believe life has no meaning beyond what you're doing today, then death will be, to you, an ugly intrusion full of bitterness.

If you believe life is a tiresome struggle weighted with failures and disappointments, then dying, for you, may be a fatal escape.

But if you accept life as a gift from God, then dying is a part of the given. You can prepare for it. You can approach it. Because you can say, "For to me, to live is Christ and to die is gain."[6]

10

Life Worth Living

To Whom It May Concern:

I hate my life. You can't imagine the ache of wanting to end your life and not being able to because you're a quadriplegic and can't use your hands.

After the doctors did surgery on my neck, I refused to wear a neck collar. I hate it too. Nobody understands and nobody will listen to me when I tell them I don't want to live. People feel sorry for me and I can't stand it. I can't even go to the bathroom by myself.

I don't have the energy to cope, I don't have the strength to face the next day. I want out.

A depressed teenager

What would you say to this teenager? What sort of advice would you give her? Now that you've come this far, I certainly hope you would not give her a copy of *Final Exit*!

It's safe to say you'd want to help. But how much time and support would you be willing to invest in her? It would take a lot of effort to sit by the hospital bedside and listen, to hold her hand, and genuinely care. She might spit abuse at you . . . she might turn her head on the pillow and sullenly ignore you . . . she might even scream at a nurse to kick you out of the room.

Could you, with supernatural love, turn the other cheek? Would you be able to care with no strings attached? Would you think to come back the next day with a *Seventeen* magazine, a package of Twinkies, and just quietly sit at her bedside to watch *Star Trek*?

That girl is one of millions—depressed, disillusioned, and crying out the unspoken question: Where is life that is worth living? Remember, the answer to that question comes not in the form of a sentence, but in people.

Finding Answers in People

The suicidal teenager who wrote the "To Whom It May Concern" letter was me. I begged my friend Jackie to bring from home her mother's sleeping pills or her father's razors. I daydreamed of the time when I could sit up in a motorized wheelchair and power it off a high curb (just my luck I would only become brain-injured and worsen my misery!). When my friend stubbornly refused, I waited at night until no nurses were around so I could thrash my head on the pillow, hoping that my neck would snap at a higher level and cut off my breathing.

I had no pride when it came to bowing out of life. The funny thing is that at one time I had said, "People who cut their lives short are weak-minded, weak-willed wimps who have spaghetti for a back-bone. Why can't they pull themselves up by their bootstraps, hold their breath, and just charge through the suffering without a lot of mopey complaining!" You'd be surprised how many people feel that way at least until they are the ones who become emotional spaghetti.

When a diving accident paralyzed more than just my body, all I wanted was to escape. Escape into daydreams. Escape into sleep. Escape into television. And if I were able, escape into death.

I am not the only one. Millions more don't want to suffer through anything, whether it be bad health, bad finances, bad pain, or bad relationships. Escape has become the great American pastime and our culture doesn't help. Our media-oriented society tries to sell us one image after the other of the good life free of pain. When a society buys into that culture of comfort, it's just a short hop philosophically into the hospital or nursing home lounges where life-and-death decisions are made. Or it's just a short hop to the local bookstore to pick up a copy of *Final Exit*.

Thankfully, I never was able to engineer that final escape.

Instead I found other answers rather than an escape hatch; those answers came in the form of people who loved me. Mrs. Miller, the mother of a high school classmate, visited my bedside once a week. I was embarrassed to show anger in front of her and, besides, she brought in home-baked sugar cookies. A boisterous and hardy high school friend named Diana gave up a semester of college to stick by my bedside. Her commitment impressed me and I liked her corny jokes. A boy named Steve loved the challenge of answering my questions about the Bible. I tolerated him because he was younger than I.

People like these took away my desperate urge to escape. In fact, I found their company much more satisfying than any escape hatch. Steve, for instance, was so caring and persistent. I'll never forget the time I cornered him and whispered half-crying, "It's so . . . hard."

He didn't say a word but picked up his guitar and sang an Elton John tune, ". . . my gift is my song and this one's for you." The words of the music contained no answers whatsoever for my despair, but the tender and innocent expression of love on his young face was all the healing I needed, at least for that moment.

Mrs. Miller, Diana, Steve, my sisters . . . these people connected me from one healing moment to the next until I had finally surfaced out of my suicidal despair. I looked back into the fog of that funereal depression and realized that I hadn't found answers, so much as I had found friends.

God Understands Too

There's hardly a soul who has ever lived who hasn't wrestled with the overwhelming urge to escape suffering, permanently. In fact, the strongest most stalwart of saints are sometimes the most likely candidates for ending it all.

Even a powerful prophet like Elijah discovered he had spaghetti for a backbone. When the wicked queen Jezebel heard through the grapevine that Elijah had wiped out hundreds of her prophets, she went after his neck. Elijah got weak-kneed and ran for his life. When he reached the desert, he gave up. He didn't even have the courage to do himself in— he begged God to perform the mercy killing on him.

"I have had enough, Lord," he said. "Take my life. . ."

Here's a curious footnote. God used Elijah to perform spectacular miracles just the day before. He had announced the end of a drought. He was the people's best friend. Elijah had nothing to complain about. Why in the world would he, of all people, want such a permanent solution for such a little bit of depression?

But that's the point. Whether you are terminally ill and on your last legs, or hunch-shouldered with a bad case of the Monday morning blues. Whether you are a grandmother facing a dead end in a nursing home, or a cerebral-palsied young man facing a similar end at the bottom of a bottle of pills. From super saints to quads like me, no one is immune.

Elijah would understand. More important, God understands. Circumstances may vary from human to human, but we can draw comfort from the fact that all of us are as vulnerable as Elijah. If you look closer at how this mighty prophet surfaced out of his suicidal despair, you'll also see that answers came to him in the form of people. Actually, a Person.

God himself ministered to the prophet. God handed him food, maybe even something as tasty as Twinkies. God gave him sleep, and I'm sure Elijah's rest was as quieting and soothing as Steve's gentle song. God even offered a listening, empathetic ear. The record shows that the angel of the Lord touched Elijah and agreed that, ". . . the journey is too much for you."[1] He then presented Elijah with new work to do, and sometimes switching focus onto others is just what the doctor would order.

How can I help you see? The lesson of Elijah is for us all. Just as surely as the angel of the Lord personally gave the prophet a sip of cool water and laid him down to rest, the Lord touches our lives through the people He places around us. Mrs. Miller and Diana, my mother, and my sisters certainly were the hands and heart of God to me. And if there is no Steve or Diana, God can personally come through for you giving you strength out of nowhere.

Elijah was able to turn the corner and get back on the track, thanks to God. I, too, knew I had turned the corner out of despair when I stopped wrenching my neck on the pillow and started to pray. My prayer during those midnight moments when the faint fragrance of friendship from my sisters, Diana, and the rest was still in the air:

"God, if I can't die ... show me how to live."

Life Is Worth Living
With the Person, Jesus Christ

A prayer like "Show me how to live" assumes
that you can see at least a few steps in front of you.
But sometimes you can't see a blessed thing. As it
says in Isaiah 50:10 (TLB), "If men walk in darkness,
without one ray of light ..."

That pretty much described Dorothy Dalenberg.
Total blackness. No way out. Darkness so thick,
there was not a single ray of light. Dorothy isn't in a
coma, doesn't live in a wheelchair, and isn't facing a
terminal illness. But her black and burdensome
circumstances are the sort most people can identify
with. Maybe even you:

Dear Joni,
I injured my neck, which resulted in chronic pain
and terrible headaches. Suddenly activities I took
for granted came at the price of pain, tears and
frustration. Pushing a grocery cart put my neck in
spasms. Cleaning the sink left me in bed with pain
pills. I was frequently incapacitated, often going to
the emergency room for pain shots.
As I fought to cope, my world unraveled. I had
sinus surgery, totaled my car, and was told I have
fibromyalgia and a glandular disease. God seemed
so distant. I could not feel the peace He promised.
I became very depressed. I wasn't living. I was
existing from pain pill to pain pill. No hope. So
tired. Gradually I decided life was not worth living.

I began to think of how I would end it all. I felt my family would be better off without me, but I hung onto their love . . . or maybe their love hung onto me.

I didn't see it at first, but God was there all along. In the friends who listened to me, cared for and accepted me. Through the care of my doctors and a Christian counselor, I learned to control my pain, not let it control me. I discovered my worth is not dependent on what I can do or how I feel. My security comes from who I am in Christ.

My life will never be the same. But, God has given me a burden to reach out to others in life's dark hours. Pain I will always have, but now I know He will never leave me nor forsake me.

Dorothy Dalenberg

Somewhere in her darkest moment Dorothy uttered a prayer not unlike mine, "Show me how to live." And Isaiah 50:10 (TLB) was handcrafted for people like her and me. "If men walk in darkness without one ray of light . . ." She felt the thick blackness, and she knew there was not a single ray of light anywhere. Some would say that's a good signal to end it all. But read the rest of the verse. It says, "If men walk in darkness without one ray of light, *let them trust the Lord, let them rely upon their God*" (Italics mine).

When Dorothy reached out in the blackness not expecting to find a thing, not even a light switch to shed some hope on her bleak circumstances, she found the hand of Someone right in the midst of her darkest hour. God showed her how to live when He showed her ... Himself.

You will only find life worth living if you reach out in the darkness to discover the hand of Christ. Maybe that's why Jesus said, "I am the light of the world." Rays of light are first and foremost found in Him.

And listen to what Jesus says not only about light, but life. He says, "Do not worry about your life. I have come that you might have life and have it more abundantly." He also says "I am the resurrection and the life. I am the way and the truth and the life." Even one of His apostles said, "Lord, to whom shall we go? You have the words of eternal life."[2]

Life is intricately and intimately linked with Jesus. In fact, Jesus is life—He said so Himself. So when we look for life worth living, we must look for it not in happy or heartbreaking circumstances, health, or even relationships. Life is in Christ. That's why Dorothy, and countless others I've mentioned, believe life is worth living. They count the courage and love, friends and smiles, patience and perseverance, poems and music, peace and hope ... they count all of this "life" that God gives, worth the pain.

Back to the Beginning

Remember when you started this book I told you about my three-week stint in bed with pressure sores? How I described the bird feeder my husband Ken hung outside our bedroom window, and the many sparrows that came and visited? I told you how my depression made me envious of the sparrows flying and fluttering so carefree.

During one of those long, dreary evenings in bed, I was reading my Bible and came across the little lecture Jesus gave on sparrows. He was speaking to His disciples about the future and when He sensed fear rising in their hearts, Jesus reassured them:

> Are not two sparrows sold for a penny? Yet not one of them will fall to the ground apart from the will of your Father. And even the very hairs of your head are all numbered. So don't be afraid; you are worth more than many sparrows.[3]

I glanced at the bird feeder and smiled. I could understand Jesus noticing an eagle or falcon or hawk falling to the ground. Those are important birds God created, the kind worth attending to. But a scrappy sparrow? They're a dime a dozen. Jesus said so Himself.

Yet from thousands of bird species, the Lord chose the most insignificant, least-noticed, scruffiest bird of all. A pint-sized thing that even dedicated birdwatchers ignore.

That thought alone calmed my fears. I felt significant and noticed. Because if God takes note of each humble sparrow—who they are, where they are, and what they're doing—I know He keeps tabs on me. For my remaining days in bed, every bird that visited the feeder served as a joyful reminder of God's concern for every detail of my life.

As I told you in the first chapter, my pressure sores are healed. I've also passed the twenty-five-year milestone of my disability; I've begun my twenty-sixth year in this wheelchair. There will inevitably be days when I'll still face fear. Worries will press in. Doubts will assault. Depression will lay me low. And you don't have to be in a wheelchair to identify.

We both will do well to remember. "Do not be afraid, little flock for your Father has been pleased to give you the kingdom."[4] If the great God of heaven concerns Himself with a ragtag little sparrow clinging to the bird feeder outside my window, He cares about you.

And Forward to the End

One day your banged-up, bruised body won't matter a whole lot. Right now it screams for your undivided attention, but if you place your trust in Christ, it will one day take a backseat. As C. H. Spurgeon says, "At present we wear our bodies on the outside and our souls on the inside. But in heaven, we shall wear our bodies on the inside and our souls on the outside."

What else could the Bible possibly mean when it says that one day we will be clothed in righteousness. We will wear our righteousness as if it were a beautiful garment. I'm sure that's why the Bible also tells you to get ready on this side of eternity as you "clothe yourself with patience."

Be patient. Don't give up. This life's not over yet. It will get better. One day you will enjoy the most perfect final exit.

> But God will redeem my life from the grave; he will surely take me to himself.
>
> Psalm 49:15

Appendix:
A Physician's Perspective

We have been exposed to the debate surrounding a right to die for three decades, as the arguments for euthanasia are presented in more palatable fashion behind ever more deceptive facades. Most recently we have seen the ambivalent manner in which society deals with physicians who assist patients in committing suicide.

I have always defined euthanasia as death by someone's choice, someone who considers the life in question no longer worth living. There is a difference between helping a person live all the life he is entitled to and prolonging the act of dying. There is also a difference between letting nature take its course in a dying life and speeding the death of an individual by whatever means and for whatever purposes, no matter how well intended.

Thirty years ago and earlier, the debate about euthanasia centered around pain that could not be relieved. Today, when it is possible, in almost every case, to relieve pain and suffering, the debate has shifted to ending the lives of those despairing of their situation, who don't want to die of their diagnosis, who know they are incurable, or who have lost self-command, dignity, or quality of life.

We have overemphasized curing, compared to caring, to our detriment. The medical tradition that has served us so well for more than 2000 years came from Hippocrates and his disciples. They had very little to offer patients except care and integrity. Among other things, the Hippocratic Oath states: "I will use treatment to help the sick according to my ability and judgment, but I will never use it to injure or wrong them."

The Hippocratic Oath has been the most enduring ethical legacy of the practice of medicine, being passed on from teacher to student, from physician to new physician, from generation to generation. The Hippocratic Oath and the tradition surrounding it served mankind well for more than two thousand years and became the medical ethics and the value system that made Western medicine the art that it has become. Only recently, since the second World War, has this noble tradition been threatened. The function of the Oath in today's society is the same as when it was first spoken. The Oath calls physicians to a higher ethical standard than that of society in general.

In the society that produced the Hippocratic Oath, the lines between physician, witch doctor, and magician had become blurred as had the line between physician and executioner. The laws of the society in which the first Hippocratic physicians took that Oath allowed them to kill, allowed abortion, and allowed them to abuse the privacy of their relations with patients.

The Oath called upon physicians not to change the laws of society; that was not their function, but to commit themselves to a higher ethical standard.

The Oath was trying to say: "I" [that is, we of the school of Hippocrates], I am above such things. Though others who call themselves physicians do these things, I will not. You can count on my being a responsible physician."

You will be well on your way to understanding the Hippocratic tradition when you understand its basic premise: The physician is a healer. Perhaps the most important aspect of the Hippocratic Oath is that it does not at any time or in any way speak of the doctor's role in the relief of human suffering. The ancient doctor of those days could cure practically nothing, and it is self-evident that he did what he could within the framework of "do no harm."

With few medications or procedures in his armamentarium, the ancient physician often succumbed to the temptation to kill, assist in suicide, and so alleviate suffering by ending it with death. This, however, was not for Hippocrates. Alleviate suffering, to be sure, but never if it threatened the sanctity of human life, the basic premise of the healing physician.

I went to medical school to learn how to save lives and alleviate suffering. I saw no tension between those points of view, because I was a

Hippocratic physician. There was an absolute pros-
cription on the taking of life. If I could heal or cure, I
would do it, but in doing that or failing that, I would
relieve the suffering of my patient.

Hippocratic medicine does not require that the
act of dying ever be prolonged. If my patient has
received all that I can do for him, and healing is not
possible, I can alleviate his suffering and still stay
well within the bound of "do no harm."

In general, people don't like slippery-slope arguments. But there is a slippery slope here. I thought
Holland would have been the last country in the
world to abandon the sanctity of life, but they have
done so. Even though assisting a patient in suicide
and euthanasia are illegal in Holland, the law has
decided to look the other way. Euthanasia advocates
have misled Americans about the satisfaction the
Dutch have with their simplistic handling of euthanasia; if a patient requests death, it is delivered in
the form of a lethal injection. The truth of the
matter is that the practice of euthanasia in Holland
has overstepped the guidelines and the standards
originally agreed upon by the Netherlands medical
society. In a few short years, second opinions about
the need for euthanasia have been abandoned.
Where a euthanasia death is reported, investigations
are few and far between. Many euthanasia deaths
are not reported, even on a death certificate. All
evidence in these matters is under the control of the
physician, and patients have been killed without
having requested death. It could happen here.

C. Everett Koop, M.D.

Notes

Chapter 1

[1]The *Today Show* transcripts, August 5, 1991.

[2]"Assigning the Blame for a Young Man's Suicide," *Time* magazine (November 18, 1991): 13.

[3]P. Marx, *And Now . . . Euthanasia*, 2d ed., Issues in Law and Medicine (Terre Haute, Indiana: National Legal Center for the Medically Dependent and Disabled, Inc., 1985).

[4]"Choosing Death," *Newsweek Magazine* (August 26, 1991): 43.

Chapter 2

[1]"Assisted Suicide Idea Isn't New, But It Still Stirs a Storm of Protest," *World Magazine* (June 16, 1990): 10.

Chapter 3

[1]Ed Bobs, "Saying Life is Not Enough, the Disabled Demand Rights and Choices," *New York Times* (January 31, 1991).

[2]Isaac Asimov, endorsement on the back cover of *Final Exit* by Derek Humphry.

[3]Chuck Colson, "It's Not Over, Debbie," *Christianity Today* (October 7, 1988): 80.

[4]*Webster's New World Dictionary*, Second College Edition (New York: Simon & Schuster, 1982).

[5]"Euthanasia: Murder or Mercy?" *Backgrounder, The Berean League*, Number 2 (March 1987): 1.

[6]"The Hemlock Manuever," *Physician Magazine* (March/April 1991): 2.

Chapter 4

[1]Charles M. Coffin, *The Complete Poetry and Selected Prose of John Donne* (New York: Random House, 1952): 441.

[2]Romans 14:7.

[3]"Euthanasia: Final Exit, Final Excuse," *First Things* (December 1991): 5.

[4]"Ten Reasons Why Washington Physicians Oppose Initiative 119," sponsored by Washington Physicians Against 119, P.O. Box 2071, Redmond, Washington 98073-2071.

[5]H. Hillhorst, V. Kragt, and A. Baanders, *Euthanasia in the Hospital*, English Translation, 1983.

[6]Derek Humphry, *Final Exit* (Eugene, Oregon: The Hemlock Society, USA, 1991): 62.

Chapter 5

[1]Viktor E. Frankl, *Man's Search for Meaning*, 3d ed. (New York: Simon & Schuster, 1984): 75, 116. (Italics mine.)

[2]Idea from James M. Wall, "In the Face of Death: Rights, Choices, Beliefs," *Christian Century* (August 21–28, 1991).

[3]"Quadriplegic Petitions Court to Let Him Die" news article, 1989.

[4]For further insight into Dr. Viktor Frankl's views on God, refer to his book, *The Unconscious God*.

[5]Luke 22:42, 44.

[6]"Judge Rules Quadriplegic Can End Life at Will," Associated Press, *Kingsport Times-News* (September 7, 1989): 4B.

[7]Idea from Erika Schuchardt, *Why Is This Happening to Me?* (Minneapolis: Augsburg Publishing House, 1989).

[8]Tens of thousands of physically disabled young adults find themselves trapped in nursing homes. The disability rights movement has fought to liberate them. In states like California, people with disabilities live in their own homes, raise families, attend school, and hold jobs. Their independent and productive living is partly the result of California's In-Home Support Services Program. It provides financial aid for housekeeping and assistance with personal needs. The case of Larry McAfee contains [this] lesson: Saving people's lives and rehabilitating them is pointless if they are denied the right and the means to control their lives.

Chapter 6

[1]Matthew 4:3, 5.

[2]John 8:44

47

47

89

47

[3]C. Samuel Storms, *To Love Mercy* (Colorado Springs, Colorado: NavPress, 1991): 9.

[4]Viktor E. Frankl, *Man's Search for Meaning*, 87–88.

[5]2 Corinthians 4:8–10, *The Living Bible*, Tyndale House.

[6]Matthew 18:8.

[7]"Deliverance from Hell," *Hemlock Quarterly* (October, 1991): 5.

[8]Psalm 139:14.

[9]Jude 6; 2 Peter 2:4. Without referencing Ezekiel 28:11–19, it is universally held among Christians that the devil is one of the fallen angels mentioned in Jude 6 and 2 Peter 2:4. It's a logical conclusion that the greatest among demons would be Satan.

[10]2 Corinthians 4:3, 4.

[11]Revelation 20:7–10.

Chapter 7

[1]Peter Kreeft, *Making Sense Out of Suffering* (Ann Arbor, Michigan: Servant Books, 1986): 143. God perfectly loves us no matter what level our spiritual maturity; however, many attest that God reserves special affection for individuals who seek Him and fear Him in the manner of the apostle John or King David, men who enjoyed a "best friend" status with God. My use of Kreeft's quote is to underscore that God is more concerned with who we become rather than what we do; thus, giving each of us, no matter what our functioning ability, the opportunity to please God whatever our vocation.

[2]2 Samuel 1:9–16, 1 Chronicles 10:4, *The Living Bible*.

[3]1 Chronicles 10:4.

[4]The real issue in this story is, indeed, not one of mercy killing, but of harming the person who is set apart for the Lord's service. David was angry that the Amalekite "destroyed the Lord's anointed." We should certainly have as much respect for the life of a chosen child of God as the Israelites did for their king.

[5]Exodus 20:13; Matthew 22:39. (Italics mine.)

[6]Judges 9:54–57; 2 Samuel 1:9–16; 1 Kings 16:15–19; Matthew 27:5.

[7]1 Corinthians 6:19, 20.

[8]Some evangelicals believe moral principles can be violated when there is a conflict of duties. However, in Scripture it is never right to disobey a command of God, and it is never sinful to do right. For further study on whether or not it is ever right to morally disobey God, see Dr. John Frame's book, *Medical Ethics* (Phillipsburg, New Jersey: Presbyterian and Reformed Publishing Company, 1988).

9"The Nightmare Nears," *Moody Monthly* editorial (January 1992): 8.

10Hebrews 2:14, 15 TLB.

111 Corinthians 15:26

12John 10:10 TLB.

13Romans 8:18.

14Psalm 39:4–6.

15Elisabeth Elliot, *Forget Me Not* (Portland, Oregon: Multnomah Press, 1989).

16Ephesians 3:10 PHILLIPS.

17Matthew 6:34.

Chapter 8

1Job 1:21.

2*Webster's New World Dictionary.*

3C. Everett Koop, *The Right to Die*, page 110.

4Proverbs 11:14 KJV.

5Deuteronomy 30:19.

6*Ethical Statement*, "Euthanasia" Christian Medical and Dental Society, May 3, 1990.

7C. Everett Koop, "The Surgeon General on Euthanasia, *Presbyterian Journal* (September 25, 1985): 8.

8Rita L. Marker, "What's All the Fuss about Tube Feeding?" *New Covenant* (January 1991): 19.

9"Euthanasia," *Ethical Statement*, Christian Medical and Dental Society (May 3, 1990).

10C. Everett Koop, "The End Is Not the End," *Christianity Today* (March 6, 1987): 18.

11Callista Gould, "Two Real Life 'Awakenings' Challenge PVS Diagnosis," *National Right to Life News* (January 1992): 34.

12Matthew 16:17.

13Luke 1:44, 45.

14Dr. John M. Frame, personal letter.

152 Corinthians 4:18.

Chapter 9

1Glen Davidson, *Living with Dying* (Minneapolis: Augsburg Publishing, 1975).

²"Durable Power of Attorney for Health Care," (California Civil Code Sections 2410–2443).
³Ecclesiastes 3:2.
⁴2 Corinthians 5:8–9.
⁵Philippians 3:20–21.
⁶Philippians 1:21.

Chapter 10

¹1 Kings 19:7–8.
²Matthew 6:25; John 10:10; John 11:25; John 6:68; John 14:6.
³Matthew 10:29–31.
⁴Luke 12:32.

Joni Eareckson Tada is affiliated with
The Christian Institute on Disability.
For information on how your church can
accelerate outreach into the disability
community, contact:

The Christian Institute on Disability
P.O. Box 3333
Agoura Hills, CA 91301